Level C
Mastering Math

Program Consultants

Robert Abbott
Assistant Director of Special Education
Waukegan Community Unit School District No. 60
Waukegan, Illinois

Marie Davis
Principal, McCoy Elementary School
Orange County Public Schools
Orlando, Florida

Monika Spindel
Mathematics Teacher
Austin, Texas

Suzanne H. Stevens
Specialist in Learning Disabilities
Learning Enhancement Consultant
Winston-Salem, North Carolina

A Harcourt Company

www.steck-vaughn.com

Table of Contents

Chapter 1: Addition and Subtraction Facts Through 18 1
   Problem Solving: Make a Drawing 16
Chapter 2: Place Value Through Thousands 23
   Problem Solving: Make a Drawing 38
Chapter 3: Addition and Subtraction with Regrouping 45
   Problem Solving: Use a Table 60
Cumulative Review: Chapters 1–3 67
Chapter 4: Multiplication Facts Through 5 75
   Problem Solving: Make a Table 90
Chapter 5: Multiplication Facts Through 9 97
   Problem Solving: Find a Pattern 112
Chapter 6: Division Facts Through 6 119
   Problem Solving: Find a Pattern 134
Cumulative Review: Chapters 4–6 141
Extra Practice:
   Chapter 1 147
   Chapter 2 149
   Chapter 3 151
   Chapter 4 153
   Chapter 5 155
   Chapter 6 157

Acknowledgments

Editorial Director
Diane Schnell

Supervising Editor
Donna Rodgers

Assistant Art Director
Cynthia Ellis

Design Manager
Sheryl Cota

Media Researcher
Claudette Landry

Contributing Writers
Brantley Eastman, Diane Crowley, Mary Hill, Louise Marinilli, Harriet Stevens, Susan Murphy, Helen Coleman, Ann McSweeney

Illustration
Rondi Collette: pages 6, 10, 11, 27, 31, 53, 76, 77, 80, 81, 84, 107, 120, 121, 126, 131, 133 David Griffin: pages 2, 3, 4, 16, 17, 22, 35, 38, 87 Maria Lyle: page 5 Linda Medina: pages 8, 9, 12, 13, 33, 79, 82, 89, 98, 101, 111, 124, 128, 129, clocks

Photography
Cover: (starfish) ©PhotoDisc, (watch) ©Michael Newman/PhotoEdit; p. 1 ©Superstock; pp. 7, 15 ©PhotoDisc; p. 23 ©Superstock; pp. 25, 37 ©PhotoDisc; p. 45 ©Tony Freeman/PhotoEdit; pp. 47, 49 ©PhotoDisc; p. 55 CORBIS/Alissa Crandall; p. 75 ©Richard Cummins/The Viesti Collection, Inc.; p. 83 ©PhotoDisc; p. 85 SV Library; p. 97 ©Index Stock Photography; pp. 103, 105 ©PhotoDisc; p. 119 ©LWA-DANN Tardif/The Stock Market; pp. 125, 127 ©PhotoDisc; Additional photography by: Digital Studios.

ISBN 0-7398-1246-7

Copyright © 2000 Steck-Vaughn Company
All rights reserved. No part of the material protected by this copyright may be reproduced in any form or by any means, electronic or mechanical, including photocopying, recording, or by any information storage and retrieval system, without permission in writing from the copyright owner. Requests for permission to make copies of any part of the work should be mailed to: Copyright Permissions, Steck-Vaughn Company, P.O. Box 26015, Austin, Texas 78755. Printed in the United States of America.

4 5 6 7 8 9 DBH 03 02 01

CHAPTER 1
Addition and Subtraction Facts Through 18

Some friends have a pet show.
There are 6 dogs and 4 cats in the show.
How many dogs and cats in all are in the show?

Solve

▶ Write your own problem about a pet show.

_____

_____

_____

_____

Adding to 10

We **add** to find out how many there are in all.

How many lions are there in all?

Step 1 Count:  and  are 5 in all.

Step 2 Write: 3 + 2 = 5   or $\begin{array}{r} 3 \\ + 2 \\ \hline 5 \end{array}$

Step 3 Say: There are 5 lions in all

The numbers we add are called **addends**. 3 and 2 are addends.
The answer is called the **sum**. 5 is the sum.

Guided Practice

▸ Add.

1. $\begin{array}{r} 4 \\ + 2 \\ \hline 6 \end{array}$	2. $\begin{array}{r} 3 \\ + 5 \\ \hline \end{array}$	3. $\begin{array}{r} 2 \\ + 0 \\ \hline \end{array}$	4. $\begin{array}{r} 8 \\ + 2 \\ \hline \end{array}$
5. 7 + 2 =	6. 1 + 3 =	7. 6 + 1 =	8. 2 + 6 =

Practice

▸ Add.

1. 4 +1	2. 3 +3	3. 9 +1	4. 3 +4
5. 6 +3	6. 3 +7	7. 4 +4	8. 8 +1
9. 5 +0	10. 7 +1	11. 5 +5	12. 2 +2
13. 2 + 1 =	14. 6 + 4 =	15. 5 + 2 =	16. 2 + 3 =

Using Math

▸ A zoo has 5 white tigers and 4 striped tigers. How many tigers are there in all?

There are _____ tigers in all.

Work here.

5
+4

3

2
Adding to 14

How many ostriches are there in all?

Step 1 Count:  and 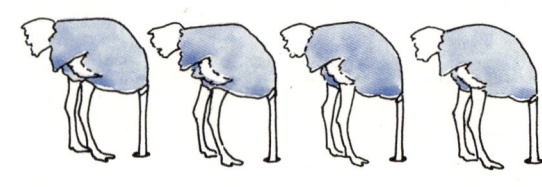 are 11 in all.

Step 2 Write: 7 + 4 = 11   or $\begin{array}{r} 7 \\ + 4 \\ \hline 11 \end{array}$

Step 3 Say: There are 11 ostriches in all.

Guided Practice

Add.

1. $\begin{array}{r} 7 \\ + 7 \\ \hline 14 \end{array}$	2. $\begin{array}{r} 9 \\ + 2 \\ \hline \end{array}$	3. $\begin{array}{r} 5 \\ + 8 \\ \hline \end{array}$	4. $\begin{array}{r} 6 \\ + 5 \\ \hline \end{array}$
5. 6 + 7 =	6. 8 + 6 =	7. 7 + 5 =	8. 9 + 4 =

Practice

▷ Add.

1. 5 + 9	2. 4 + 8	3. 5 + 4	4. 9 + 3
5. 7 + 4	6. 2 + 5	7. 4 + 9	8. 5 + 7
9. 8 + 3	10. 6 + 8	11. 3 + 9	12. 5 + 6
13. 7 + 6 =	14. 3 + 8 =	15. 9 + 5 =	16. 4 + 0 =

Using Math

▷ The zoo has 6 polar bears and 6 black bears. How many bears are there in all?

There are ____ bears in all.

Work here.

5

Adding to 18

How many butterflies are there in all?

Step 1 Count:  and  are 15 in all.

Step 2 Write: 9 + 6 = 15   or $\begin{array}{r} 9 \\ + 6 \\ \hline 15 \end{array}$

Step 3 Say: There are 15 butterflies in all.

Guided Practice

▸ Add.

1. $\begin{array}{r} 8 \\ + 7 \\ \hline 15 \end{array}$	2. $\begin{array}{r} 7 \\ + 9 \\ \hline \end{array}$	3. $\begin{array}{r} 9 \\ + 9 \\ \hline \end{array}$	4. $\begin{array}{r} 9 \\ + 6 \\ \hline \end{array}$
5. 8 + 8 =	6. 6 + 9 =	7. 9 + 8 =	8. 8 + 7 =

Practice

Add.

1. 9 + 8	2. 8 + 8	3. 9 + 6	4. 9 + 7
5. 8 + 9	6. 4 + 6	7. 2 + 7	8. 5 + 3
9. 4 + 3	10. 9 + 4	11. 2 + 9	12. 4 + 7
13. 7 + 6 =	14. 7 + 8 =	15. 9 + 5 =	16. 8 + 9 =

Using Math

There are 9 daisies and 7 tulips.
How many flowers are there in all?

There are _____ flowers in all.

Work here.

4

Subtraction Facts Through 10

We **subtract** to find out how many are left.

How many birds are left?

Step 1 Count: 4

Step 2 Subtract:

Step 3 Write: 4 − 2 = 2   or

Step 4 Say: There are 2 birds left.

The answer of a subtraction problem is called the **difference**.
2 is the difference.

Guided Practice

Subtract.

1. $\begin{array}{r}6\\-4\\\hline 2\end{array}$	2. $\begin{array}{r}8\\-3\\\hline\end{array}$	3. $\begin{array}{r}4\\-0\\\hline\end{array}$	4. $\begin{array}{r}10\\-2\\\hline\end{array}$
5. 9 − 2 =	6. 10 − 4 =	7. 5 − 4 =	8. 7 − 3 =

Practice

▸ Subtract.

1. 8 − 4	2. 8 − 6	3. 6 − 3	4. 5 − 5
5. 7 − 5	6. 3 − 3	7. 10 − 1	8. 9 − 4
9. 8 − 1	10. 10 − 5	11. 3 − 2	12. 7 − 0
13. 7 − 6 =	14. 9 − 1 =	15. 10 − 3 =	16. 9 − 6 =

Using Math

▸ There are 5 seals. 3 swim away. How many are left?

_____ seals are left.

Work here.

5
− 3

9

Subtraction Facts Through 14

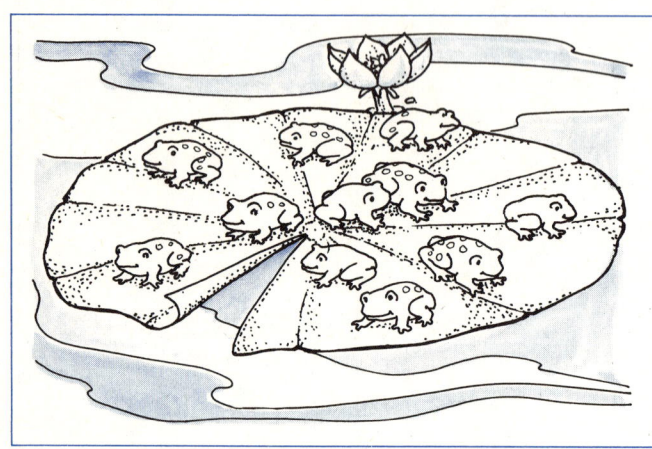

How many frogs are left?

Step 1 Count: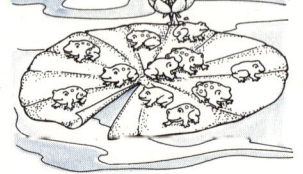

Step 2 Subtract:

Step 3 Write: 11 − 6 = 5   or $\begin{array}{r}11\\-6\\\hline 5\end{array}$

Step 4 Say: There are 5 frogs left.

Guided Practice

▸ Subtract.

1. $\begin{array}{r}11\\-9\\\hline 2\end{array}$	2. $\begin{array}{r}14\\-6\\\hline\end{array}$	3. $\begin{array}{r}12\\-5\\\hline\end{array}$	4. $\begin{array}{r}14\\-8\\\hline\end{array}$
5. 14 − 7 =	6. 11 − 8 =	7. 12 − 3 =	8. 13 − 5 =

10

Practice

▶ Subtract.

1. 12 -6	2. 14 -5	3. 13 -8	4. 13 -7
5. 11 -4	6. 12 -9	7. 5 -2	8. 13 -6
9. 12 -4	10. 11 -3	11. 12 -7	12. 13 -4
13. $13 - 9 =$	14. $11 - 7 =$	15. $12 - 8 =$	16. $14 - 9 =$

Using Math

▶ There are 14 bees around the hive. 7 fly away. How many bees are left?

_____ bees are left.

Work here.

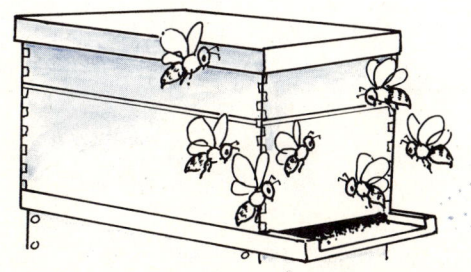

11

Subtraction Facts Through 18

How many ducks are left?

Step 1 Count:

Step 2 Subtract:

Step 3 Write: $15 - 9 = 6$ or $\begin{array}{r} 15 \\ -9 \\ \hline 6 \end{array}$

Step 4 Say: There are 6 ducks left.

Guided Practice

▷ Subtract.

1. $\begin{array}{r}16\\-7\\\hline 9\end{array}$	2. $\begin{array}{r}15\\-8\\\hline\end{array}$	3. $\begin{array}{r}17\\-9\\\hline\end{array}$	4. $\begin{array}{r}17\\-8\\\hline\end{array}$
5. $18 - 9 =$	6. $16 - 8 =$	7. $15 - 6 =$	8. $16 - 9 =$

12

Practice

▶ Subtract.

1. 18 − 9	2. 16 − 9	3. 15 − 7	4. 15 − 9
5. 16 − 8	6. 10 − 2	7. 7 − 4	8. 9 − 7
9. 8 − 2	10. 14 − 6	11. 15 − 6	12. 11 − 7
13. 11 − 2 =	14. 17 − 8 =	15. 13 − 5 =	16. 15 − 7 =

Using Math

▶ There are 17 ladybugs in the garden. 8 fly away. How many are left?

_____ ladybugs are left.

Work here.

Days of the Week

There are 7 **days** in a **week**. Each day has its own place in the week. The following chart shows the order of the days of the week.

| Sunday | Monday | Tuesday | Wednesday | Thursday | Friday | Saturday |

Sunday is the first day of the week. What day comes after Sunday? Can you tell what day comes before Sunday?

Guided Practice

▸ Use the chart to fill in the blanks.

1. The day before Tuesday is ____Monday____.

2. The day after Tuesday is _____.

3. The day before Saturday is _____.

4. The day after Saturday is _____.

5. The day after Thursday is _____.

6. The day before Sunday is _____.

7. The day after Sunday is _____.

8. The day after Wednesday is _____.

Practice

▷ Use the chart to fill in the blanks.

1. The day after Monday is _____.

2. The day before Wednesday is _____.

3. The day before Sunday is _____.

4. The day after Thursday is _____.

5. The day before Monday is _____.

6. The day before Friday is _____.

7. The day after Sunday is _____.

8. The day before Thursday is _____.

9. The day after Wednesday is _____.

10. The day before Saturday is _____.

Using Math

▷ Lee's family is coming home from vacation on the day after Friday. What day of the week are they coming home?

They are coming home on _____.

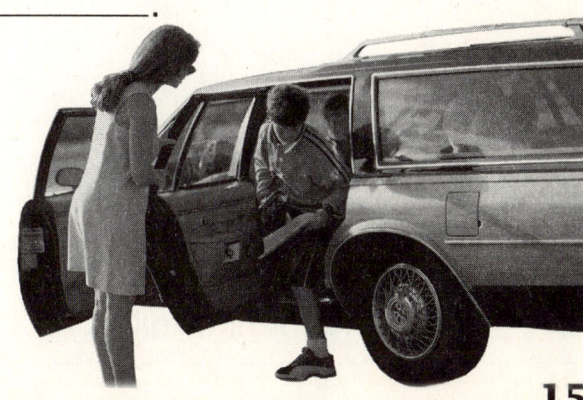

Problem Solving

Make a Drawing

Ryan has 7 baseball cards.
He will buy 5 more cards next week.
He makes a drawing to show how many baseball cards he will have then.

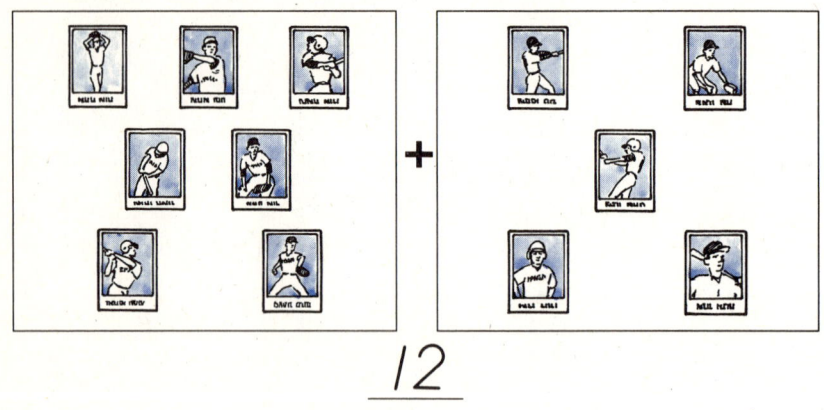

_12_

Ryan drew 7 cards.
Then he drew 5 cards.

Then Ryan counted
12 baseball cards in all.

Guided Practice

▶ Make a drawing to solve.

1. Sarah made 3 pot holders for her mother. She made 4 pot holders for her uncle. How many pot holders in all did she make?

   [ ] + [ ]

   _____ pot holders in all

2. Mark wrote 6 thank-you notes after his birthday party. He will write 6 more notes. How many in all will he write?

   [ ] + [ ]

   _____ thank-you notes in all

Practice

▶ Make a drawing to solve.

1. Luis planted 7 flowers in one pot and 8 flowers in another pot. How many flowers in all does he have?

_____ flowers in all

2. Ms. Lewis had 9 red pencils in one box and 9 black pencils in another box. How many pencils in all did she have?

_____ pencils in all

3. Ming set 5 red model cars on one shelf. She placed 4 blue model cars on another shelf. How many model cars in all are there?

_____ model cars in all

4. Justin had 9 books on the top shelf. He had 8 books on the bottom shelf. How many books in all were on these shelves?

_____ books in all

CHAPTER  **Review**

▶ Add.

pages 2–3			
1. 2 + 4	2. 3 + 0	3. 6 + 3	4. 2 + 2
5. 8 + 2	6. 4 + 4	7. 2 + 5	8. 4 + 1
pages 4–5 9. 6 + 8	10. 7 + 4	11. 8 + 5	12. 9 + 5
13. 6 + 7	14. 3 + 9	15. 5 + 6	16. 7 + 5
pages 6–7 17. 8 + 8	18. 9 + 8	19. 7 + 9	20. 7 + 8
21. 6 + 9	22. 8 + 7	23. 9 + 9	24. 8 + 9

CHAPTER 1 Review

▸ Subtract.

pages 8–9			
25. 8 − 4	26. 10 − 7	27. 9 − 5	28. 7 − 2
pages 10–11			
29. 13 − 9	30. 11 − 2	31. 12 − 5	32. 14 − 5
33. 14 − 8	34. 11 − 8	35. 12 − 8	36. 13 − 6
pages 12–13			
37. 18 − 9	38. 17 − 8	39. 15 − 9	40. 16 − 7
41. 15 − 7	42. 16 − 9	43. 16 − 8	44. 17 − 9

▸ Write the day that completes each sentence.   pages 14–15

45. The day before Monday is _____.
      Sunday   Friday

46. The day after Wednesday is _____.
      Tuesday   Thursday

19

CHAPTER 1 Review

Make a drawing to solve.
pages 16–17

47. Rita put 8 short nails in a bag. She put 6 long nails in another bag. How many nails in all does she have?

☐ + ☐

_____ nails in all

48. Steve used 4 eggs in a cake. He used 3 eggs in cookies. How many eggs in all did he use?

☐ + ☐

_____ eggs in all

49. Katie planted 9 flowers by the mailbox. She planted 5 flowers by the sidewalk. How many flowers in all did she plant?

☐ + ☐

_____ flowers in all

50. Jill had 7 fish in an aquarium. She bought 4 more fish to put in the aquarium. How many fish in all did she have then?

☐ + ☐

_____ fish in all

CHAPTER  **Test**

▸Add.

1. 9 + 4	2. 8 + 3	3. 7 + 5	4. 6 + 2
5. 8 + 9	6. 9 + 7	7. 7 + 8	8. 9 + 9

▸Subtract.

9. 9 − 3	10. 8 − 5	11. 10 − 6	12. 7 − 4
13. 14 − 5	14. 13 − 7	15. 11 − 6	16. 12 − 8
17. 15 − 6	18. 17 − 9	19. 16 − 7	20. 15 − 8

▸Write the day that completes each sentence.

21. The day before Saturday is _____.
                                       Thursday   Friday

22. The day after Monday is _____.
                                  Tuesday   Sunday

CHAPTER 1 Test

▸ Make a drawing to solve.

23. Matt drew 6 stars on a picture. Diane drew 5 stars on a picture. How many stars in all did they draw?

☐ + ☐

_____ stars in all

24. Wang put 7 chocolate doughnuts in a box. He put 5 plain doughnuts in a box. How many doughnuts in all did he have?

☐ + ☐

_____ doughnuts in all

25. Gina put 8 cans of beans on the shelf. She put 9 cans of corn on the shelf. How many cans in all did she put on the shelf?

_____ cans in all

26. Sam put 6 square blocks on a shelf. He put 3 rectangle blocks on a shelf. How many blocks in all did he put on the shelf?

_____ blocks in all

CHAPTER 2
Place Value Through Thousands

The number of chickens in Farmer Day's yard is 4 hundreds 6 tens 8 ones. Write a 3-digit number to show how many chickens are in the yard.

Solve

▷ Write a problem about a farm using hundreds, tens, and ones.

_____
_____
_____

Tens and Ones

10 ones   equal   1 ten

3 tens 4 ones = | tens | ones |
| --- | --- |
| 3 | 4 |
= 34 thirty-four

4 tens 3 ones = | tens | ones |
| --- | --- |
| 4 | 3 |
= 43 forty-three

Guided Practice

▶ Write each number.

1.
5 tens 2 ones = __52__
2 tens 5 ones = __25__

2.
4 tens 0 ones = _____
0 tens 4 ones = _____

3.
2 tens 8 ones = _____
8 tens 2 ones = _____

4.
3 tens 7 ones = _____
7 tens 3 ones = _____

5.
6 tens 0 ones = _____
0 tens 6 ones = _____

6.
1 ten 9 ones = _____
9 tens 1 one = _____

Practice

▸ Write each number.

1. 2 tens 3 ones = _____
2. 7 tens 0 ones = _____
3. 4 tens 9 ones = _____
4. 1 ten 6 ones = _____
5. 8 tens 5 ones = _____
6. 3 tens 4 ones = _____
7. 2 tens 0 ones = _____
8. 5 tens 7 ones = _____
9. 6 tens 8 ones = _____
10. 9 tens 0 ones = _____
11. 1 ten 2 ones = _____
12. 7 tens 6 ones = _____
13. 5 tens 3 ones = _____
14. 2 tens 9 ones = _____
15. 8 tens 0 ones = _____
16. 3 tens 8 ones = _____
17. 9 tens 5 ones = _____
18. 6 tens 1 one = _____
19. 2 tens 7 ones = _____
20. 4 tens 0 ones = _____
21. 0 tens 2 ones = _____
22. 6 tens 7 ones = _____
23. 1 ten 9 ones = _____
24. 9 tens 3 ones = _____
25. 4 tens 6 ones = _____
26. 5 tens 5 ones = _____

Using Math

▸ Look at the sign. Write the number as tens and ones.

_____ tens _____ ones

Hundreds, Tens, and Ones

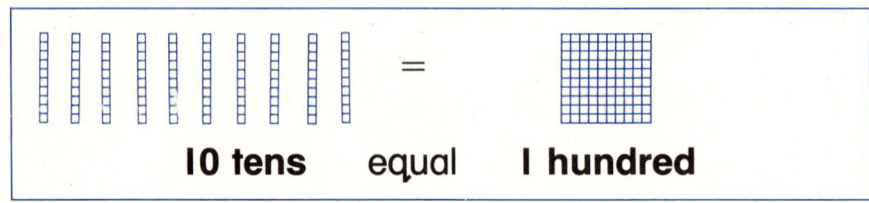

10 tens   equal   1 hundred

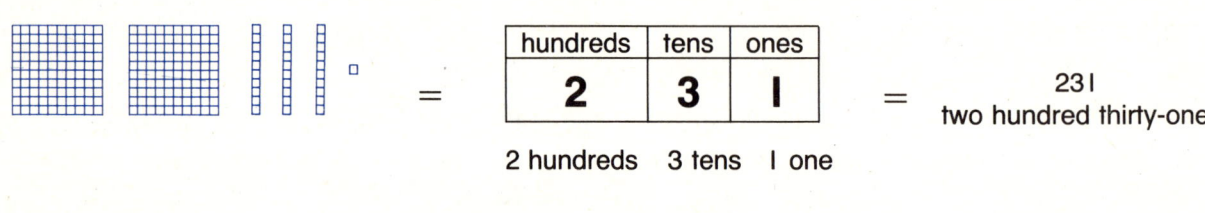

Guided Practice

▶ Write each number.

1. 1 hundred 4 tens 6 ones = __146__ 4 hundreds 1 ten 6 ones = __416__	2. 3 hundreds 7 tens 0 ones = _____ 7 hundreds 0 tens 3 ones = _____
3. 4 hundreds 5 tens 8 ones = _____ 8 hundreds 4 tens 5 ones = _____	4. 2 hundreds 0 tens 9 ones = _____ 9 hundreds 2 tens 0 ones = _____
5. 1 hundred 9 tens 7 ones = _____ 7 hundreds 1 ten 9 ones = _____	6. 5 hundreds 8 tens 6 ones = _____ 6 hundreds 8 tens 5 ones = _____

Practice

Write each number.

1. 4 hundreds 1 ten 9 ones = ____
2. 7 hundreds 2 tens 5 ones = ____
3. 6 hundreds 3 tens 8 ones = ____
4. 2 hundreds 0 tens 4 ones = ____
5. 5 hundreds 9 tens 7 ones = ____
6. 8 hundreds 5 tens 3 ones = ____
7. 1 hundred 6 tens 0 ones = ____
8. 9 hundreds 4 tens 2 ones = ____
9. 3 hundreds 7 tens 1 one = ____
10. 2 hundreds 8 tens 6 ones = ____
11. 1 hundred 4 tens 5 ones = ____
12. 7 hundreds 0 tens 9 ones = ____
13. 8 hundreds 3 tens 2 ones = ____
14. 5 hundreds 6 tens 4 ones = ____
15. 6 hundreds 9 tens 3 ones = ____
16. 4 hundreds 1 ten 0 ones = ____
17. 9 hundreds 0 tens 8 ones = ____
18. 1 hundred 5 tens 7 ones = ____
19. 2 hundreds 3 tens 6 ones = ____
20. 3 hundreds 4 tens 0 ones = ____
21. 5 hundreds 3 tens 1 one = ____
22. 8 hundreds 0 tens 4 ones = ____

Using Math

Look at the list of school supplies. How many sheets of paper are needed? ____

Write this number as hundreds, tens, and ones.

____ hundred ____ tens ____ ones

School Supplies
notebook paper (150 sheets)
5 pencils
2 pens

Expanded Form Through Hundreds

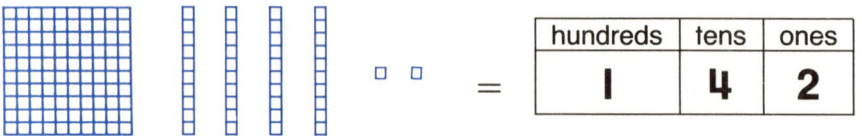

You can write 142 in **expanded form.**

1 in the **hundreds'** place = 100
4 in the **tens'** place = 40
2 in the **ones'** place = 2

100 + 40 + 2 = 142
expanded form

Guided Practice

▶ Write each number.

1. 300 + 70 + 6 = __376__ 600 + 30 + 7 = __637__	2. 800 + 90 + 4 = _____ 900 + 80 + 4 = _____
3. 500 + 2 = _____ 200 + 5 = _____	4. 600 + 80 + 1 = _____ 100 + 80 + 6 = _____
5. 900 + 30 = _____ 300 + 90 = _____	6. 700 + 50 + 8 = _____ 800 + 70 + 5 = _____

28

Practice

▶ Write each number.

1. 200 + 10 + 9 = _____
2. 400 + 60 + 3 = _____
3. 100 + 7 = _____
4. 800 + 20 + 5 = _____
5. 300 + 40 + 6 = _____
6. 700 + 9 = _____
7. 200 + 50 = _____
8. 600 + 10 + 8 = _____
9. 500 + 70 + 4 = _____
10. 900 + 20 + 3 = _____
11. 100 + 60 + 7 = _____
12. 400 + 80 = _____
13. 300 + 90 + 2 = _____
14. 500 + 40 + 1 = _____
15. 700 + 30 + 6 = _____
16. 900 + 8 = _____
17. 200 + 10 + 5 = _____
18. 400 + 70 = _____
19. 600 + 50 + 3 = _____
20. 800 + 2 = _____
21. 400 + 20 + 1 = _____
22. 300 + 50 + 9 = _____
23. 100 + 80 + 8 = _____
24. 900 + 60 = _____
25. 200 + 40 + 3 = _____
26. 700 + 90 + 5 = _____

Using Math

▶ The sign tells how many miles it is to Boston. Write this number in expanded form.

_____ + _____ + _____

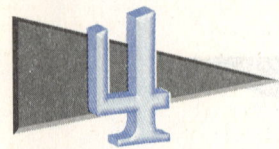

Thousands

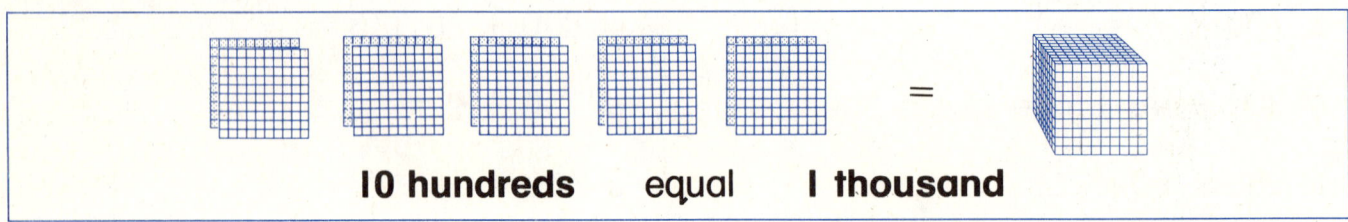

10 hundreds   equal   1 thousand

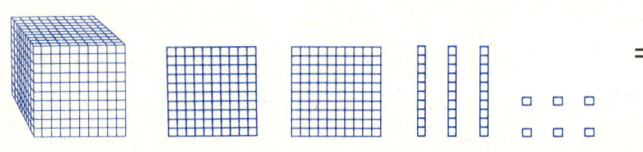 =

thousands	hundreds	tens	ones
1 ,	2	3	6

1 thousand   2 hundreds   3 tens   6 ones

1,236

one thousand two hundred thirty-six

We use a **comma** to separate the thousands from the hundreds.

Guided Practice

▶ Write each number.

1. 2 thousands 9 hundreds 0 tens 7 ones = __2,907__

   9 thousands 0 hundreds 7 tens 2 ones = __9,072__

2. 3 thousands 8 hundreds 5 tens 7 ones = _____

   8 thousands 7 hundreds 3 tens 5 ones = _____

3. 2 thousands 1 hundred 4 tens 8 ones = _____

   1 thousand 4 hundreds 8 tens 2 ones = _____

4. 5 thousands 4 hundreds 1 ten 9 ones = _____

   4 thousands 1 hundred 9 tens 5 ones = _____

Practice

Write each number.

1. 4 thousands 5 hundreds 2 tens 8 ones = _____
2. 6 thousands 0 hundreds 9 tens 7 ones = _____
3. 1 thousand 3 hundreds 8 tens 4 ones = _____
4. 5 thousands 9 hundreds 6 tens 2 ones = _____
5. 3 thousands 7 hundreds 0 tens 1 one = _____
6. 8 thousands 6 hundreds 3 tens 9 ones = _____
7. 2 thousands 1 hundred 4 tens 5 ones = _____
8. 9 thousands 2 hundreds 7 tens 0 ones = _____
9. 7 thousands 4 hundreds 1 ten 3 ones = _____
10. 1 thousand 8 hundreds 5 tens 6 ones = _____
11. 4 thousands 2 hundreds 9 tens 0 ones = _____
12. 3 thousands 0 hundreds 7 tens 5 ones = _____

Using Math

Tom has a new car. The meter in the picture shows how far he has driven it.
Write the number of miles as thousands, hundreds, tens, and ones.

_____ thousand _____ hundreds _____ tens _____ ones

31

Expanded Form Through Thousands

You can write numbers in the thousands in expanded form.

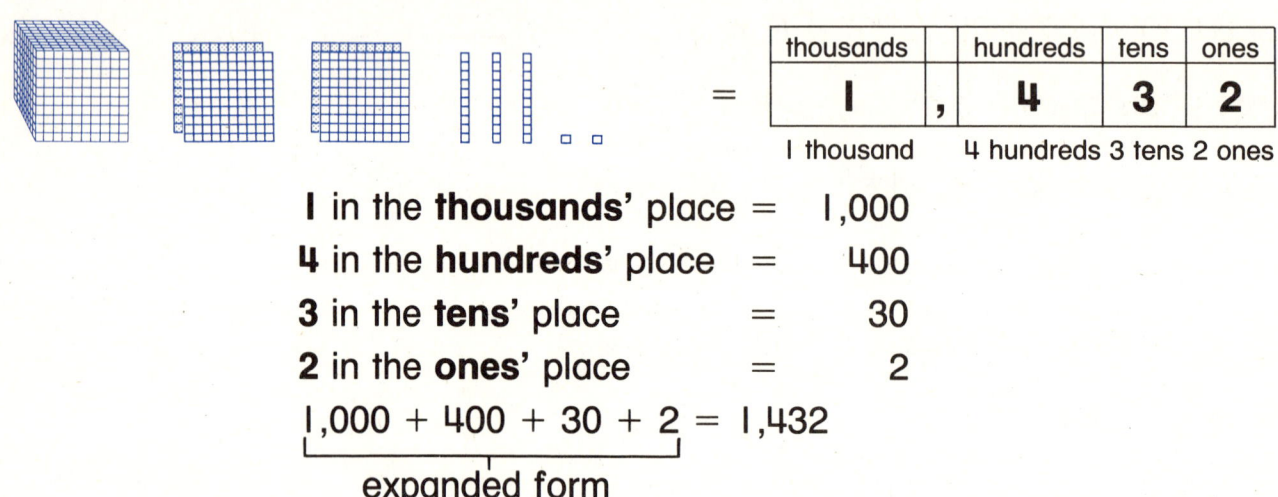

1,000 + 400 + 30 + 2 = 1,432

expanded form

Guided Practice

▶ Write each number.

1. 2,000 + 50 + 8 = __2,058__ 5,000 + 800 + 20 = __5,820__	2. 1,000 + 300 + 40 + 6 = _____ 6,000 + 400 + 30 + 1 = _____
3. 7,000 + 600 + 90 + 5 = _____ 9,000 + 700 + 50 + 6 = _____	4. 8,000 + 700 + 2 = _____ 2,000 + 70 + 8 = _____
5. 9,000 + 500 + 40 + 1 = _____ 1,000 + 400 + 50 + 9 = _____	6. 3,000 + 900 + 60 + 7 = _____ 6,000 + 700 + 90 + 3 = _____

Practice

Write each number.

1. 4,000 + 800 + 20 + 9 = _____
2. 1,000 + 500 + 3 = _____
3. 6,000 + 70 + 8 = _____
4. 2,000 + 300 + 40 + 6 = _____
5. 5,000 + 900 + 10 + 7 = _____
6. 3,000 + 2 = _____
7. 9,000 + 400 + 50 = _____
8. 7,000 + 100 + 30 + 4 = _____
9. 8,000 + 200 + 60 + 1 = _____
10. 5,000 + 700 = _____
11. 4,000 + 600 + 90 + 5 = _____
12. 2,000 + 80 = _____
13. 1,000 + 300 + 70 = _____
14. 6,000 + 400 + 10 + 9 = _____
15. 8,000 + 20 + 6 = _____
16. 7,000 + 900 + 40 + 3 = _____
17. 3,000 + 100 + 8 = _____
18. 9,000 + 200 + 60 + 7 = _____
19. 4,000 + 5 = _____
20. 1,000 + 700 + 30 + 2 = _____
21. 9,000 + 300 + 20 + 2 = _____
22. 2,000 + 600 + 5 = _____
23. 7,000 + 500 + 40 + 1 = _____
24. 5,000 + 80 + 3 = _____

Using Math

Ramona's family went on a trip. They traveled 3,298 miles from Boston to Los Angeles.
Write 3,298 in expanded form.

_____ + _____ + _____ + _____

Comparing Numbers

You can compare numbers to see which has the greater value.

Step 1 Line up the digits.

Step 2 Start at the left. Compare.

tens	ones
2	4
3	6

3 tens are greater than 2 tens, so 36 **is greater than** 24.

tens	ones
4	8
4	2

4 tens are the same. 8 ones are greater than 2 ones, so 48 **is greater than** 42.

> means **is greater than**.
36 > 24   48 > 42

< means **is less than**.
24 < 36   42 < 48

Guided Practice

Ring **greater** or **less**. Then ring > or <.

1. 17 is greater / (less) than 27
   17   > / (<)   27

2. 52 is greater / less than 49
   52   > / <   49

3. 102 is greater / less than 120
   102   > / <   120

4. 359 is greater / less than 259
   359   > / <   259

34

Practice

▷ Compare. Ring > or <.

1. 38 >/< 42	2. 76 >/< 67	3. 59 >/< 55
4. 19 >/< 21	5. 86 >/< 84	6. 29 >/< 39
7. 74 >/< 47	8. 89 >/< 91	9. 66 >/< 56
10. 22 >/< 33	11. 140 >/< 104	12. 576 >/< 579
13. 628 >/< 638	14. 213 >/< 312	15. 496 >/< 494
16. 751 >/< 715	17. 324 >/< 342	18. 857 >/< 854

Problem Solving

▷ Make a drawing to solve. Lynn drew 7 apples on a tree. Ryan drew 6 apples on a tree. How many apples in all did they draw?

_____ apples in all

Reading a Calendar

A **calendar** shows the days of the week. It also shows the **months** of the **year** in order. The numbers on a calendar tell the **dates** in order.

July

Sunday	Monday	Tuesday	Wednesday	Thursday	Friday	Saturday
			1	2	3	4
5	6	7	8	9	10	11
12	13	14	15	16	17	18
19	20	21	22	23	24	25
26	27	28	29	30	31	

This calendar shows the month of July. The first Saturday is July 4.

Guided Practice

▶ Use the July calendar to answer each question.

1. What day of the week is July 14?   __Tuesday__

2. On what day does July begin?   _____

3. How many Thursdays are there in July?   _____

4. What is the date before July 10?   _____

5. What is the date of the third Thursday?   _____

36

Practice

▶ Use the calendar on page 36 to answer each question.

1. What is the date of the last Monday? _____
2. What is the date of the first Tuesday? _____
3. What is the date of the fifth Wednesday? _____
4. What is the date of the third Monday? _____
5. What is the date of the second Sunday? _____
6. What is the date of the fourth Friday? _____
7. On what day does July end? _____
8. What day of the week is July 4? _____
9. What is the date before July 19? _____
10. What is the date of the second Saturday? _____
11. What is the date of the third Friday? _____
12. How many Mondays are there in July? _____

Using Math

▶ Julie's family is going on vacation on Saturday, July 11. The next day John's family is going on vacation. Write the day and date that John's family is leaving.

John's family is leaving on _____.

8 Problem Solving

Make a Drawing

Amy went for a walk.
She walked 4 blocks to the store.
Then she walked 7 more blocks to the park.
How far did Amy walk?

▸ Make a drawing to show where Amy went.

Make a mark on the line to show each block.
Count the blocks.
Amy is 11 blocks from home.   Answer __11__ blocks.

Guided Practice

▸ Make a drawing to solve.

1. James rode his bicycle 10 blocks to Ben's house.
   Then he rode 4 blocks back toward home to Mark's house.
   How far is James from home?

   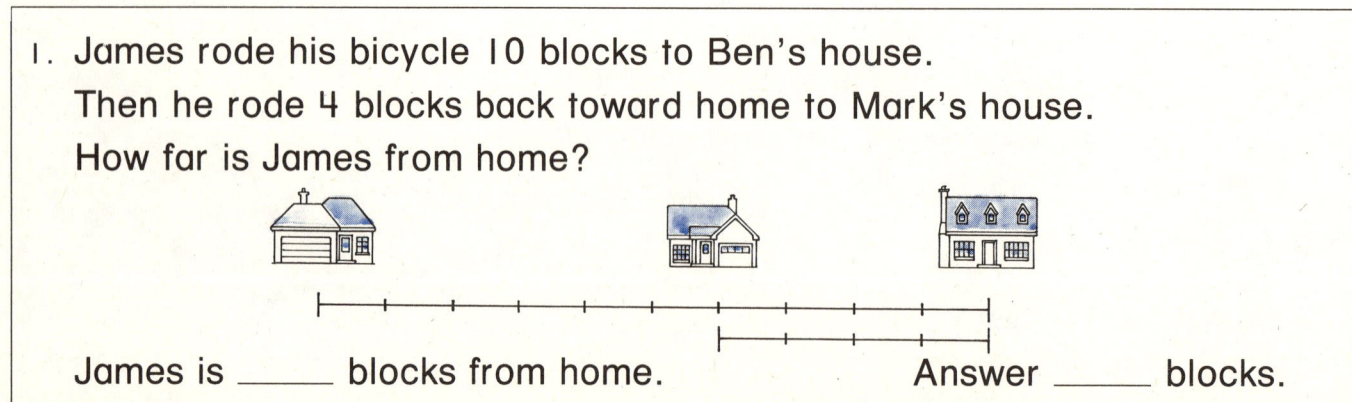

   James is _____ blocks from home.   Answer _____ blocks.

Practice

▷ Make a drawing to solve.

1. Jan rode her bike 3 blocks from her house to school.
   After school she rode 6 more blocks to the library.
   How far is the library from Jan's house?

   Answer _____ blocks.

2. David and Adam walked home from the park together.
   At the corner, David turned left and walked 2 blocks to his house.
   Adam turned right and walked 4 blocks to his house.
   How many blocks apart do David and Adam live?

   Answer _____ blocks.

3. Sue walked 11 blocks from her house to Tao's house.
   Then she walked 2 blocks back toward home to John's house.
   How far is Sue from her house?

   Answer _____ blocks.

4. Michael and Rosa walked 7 blocks to the park.
   Later they walked home the same way.
   How many blocks in all did they walk?

   Answer _____ blocks.

CHAPTER 2 Review

Write each number. pages 24–25

1. 5 tens 9 ones = _____
2. 1 ten 2 ones = _____
3. 8 tens 0 ones = _____
4. 3 tens 6 ones = _____
5. 0 tens 4 ones = _____
6. 7 tens 7 ones = _____

pages 26–27

7. 1 hundred 6 tens 8 ones = _____
8. 5 hundreds 4 tens 2 ones = _____
9. 3 hundreds 0 tens 9 ones = _____
10. 7 hundreds 8 tens 0 ones = _____
11. 4 hundreds 2 tens 6 ones = _____
12. 2 hundreds 1 ten 3 ones = _____

pages 28–29

13. 200 + 50 + 1 = _____
14. 900 + 30 = _____
15. 500 + 2 = _____
16. 300 + 10 + 8 = _____
17. 600 + 40 + 6 = _____
18. 100 + 7 = _____

pages 30–31

19. 2 thousands 0 hundreds 4 tens 0 ones = _____
20. 7 thousands 6 hundreds 1 ten 9 ones = _____
21. 5 thousands 3 hundreds 8 tens 2 ones = _____
22. 8 thousands 7 hundreds 0 tens 1 one = _____
23. 9 thousands 0 hundreds 5 tens 4 ones = _____
24. 6 thousands 2 hundreds 3 tens 6 ones = _____

pages 32–33

25. 1,000 + 200 + 50 + 3 = _____
26. 4,000 + 900 + 6 = _____
27. 3,000 + 70 + 8 = _____
28. 2,000 + 100 + 90 + 5 = _____
29. 5,000 + 40 + 2 = _____
30. 8,000 + 300 + 4 = _____

CHAPTER 2 Review

▶ Compare. Ring > or <.   pages 34–35

31. 52 > < 47	32. 67 > < 76	33. 129 > < 139
34. 126 > < 129	35. 387 > < 287	36. 546 > < 465

▶ Use the October calendar to answer each question.   pages 36–37

October

Sunday	Monday	Tuesday	Wednesday	Thursday	Friday	Saturday
				1	2	3
4	5	6	7	8	9	10
11	12	13	14	15	16	17
18	19	20	21	22	23	24
25	26	27	28	29	30	31

37. How many days are there in October? _____

38. How many Fridays are there in October? _____

39. What day of the week is October 19? _____

40. What is the date of the second Wednesday? _____

41. What is the date before October 23? _____

42. On what day does October begin? _____

CHAPTER 2 Review

▶ **Make a drawing to solve.**
pages 38–39

43. Jeff walked 6 blocks to Allan's house.
    They both walked 4 blocks to the movie theater.
    How many blocks in all did Jeff walk?

    _____   Answer _____ blocks.

44. The ice cream store is 9 blocks from Amy's house.
    Amy walked 7 blocks.
    How many more blocks does she need to walk
    to get to the ice cream store?

    _____   Answer _____ blocks.

45. Jim walked 6 blocks to Lee's house.
    Then he walked 6 more blocks to Ellen's house.
    How many blocks in all did he walk?

    _____   Answer _____ blocks.

46. Cindy rode her bike 5 blocks to the store.
    She forgot her money and rode home again.
    How many blocks in all did she ride?

    _____   Answer _____ blocks.

CHAPTER 2 Test

▶ Write each number.

1. 4 tens 8 ones = _____

2. 6 tens 0 ones = _____

3. 2 hundreds 0 tens 5 ones = _____

4. 9 hundreds 1 ten 7 ones = _____

5. 600 + 80 = _____

6. 500 + 90 + 3 = _____

7. 1 thousand 8 hundreds 2 tens 6 ones = _____

8. 4 thousands 0 hundreds 7 tens 5 ones = _____

9. 2,000 + 700 + 90 = _____

10. 5,000 + 600 + 3 = _____

▶ Compare. Ring > or <.

11. 23 > < 32

12. 249 > < 149

13. 842 > < 824

▶ Use the February calendar to answer each question.

Sunday	Monday	Tuesday	Wednesday	Thursday	Friday	Saturday
1	2	3	4	5	6	7
8	9	10	11	12	13	14
15	16	17	18	19	20	21
22	23	24	25	26	27	28

February

14. On what day does February end? _____

15. What is the date before February 15? _____

Test

▶ Make a drawing to solve.

16. Casey roller skated 5 blocks to Deanne's house.
    She roller skated back toward her house 2 blocks to go to the park.
    How far is the park from Casey's house?

    Answer _____ blocks.

17. Charlie lives 8 blocks from the zoo.
    He walked 3 blocks toward the zoo.
    How many more blocks did Charlie walk to the zoo?

    Answer _____ blocks.

18. Alice walked 9 blocks to the park.
    She walked 6 more blocks to Ann's house.
    How many blocks in all did she walk?

    Answer _____ blocks.

19. Tia rode her bike 3 blocks to Jean's house.
    Both girls rode their bikes 7 blocks to the lake.
    How many blocks in all did Tia ride her bike?

    Answer _____ blocks.

CHAPTER

Addition and Subtraction with Regrouping

Joseph collected 87 cans and bottles for recycling. His sister Sarah collected 95. How many cans and bottles in all did the brother and sister collect?

Solve

▶ Write your own problem about recycling.

45

Adding 2-Digit Numbers

Sometimes you need to **regroup** to add.

Step 1 Add the ones.

6 ones + 9 ones = 15 ones
Regroup 15 ones as 1 ten 5 ones.
Write 5 in the ones' place.
Write 1 in the tens' column.

tens	ones
1	
2	6
+ 1	9
	5

Step 2 Add the tens.

2 tens + 1 ten = 3 tens
Add 3 tens to 1 ten to get 4 tens.
Write 4 in the tens' place.

tens	ones
1	
2	6
+ 1	9
4	5

Guided Practice

▶ Add.

1. 13 + 17 = 30	2. 18 + 34	3. 35 + 26	4. 28 + 41	5. 17 + 25
6. 46 + 27	7. 58 + 26	8. 33 + 48	9. 74 + 18	10. 36 + 13

Practice

▸ Add.

1. 32 + 16	2. 45 + 17	3. 24 + 35	4. 36 + 38	5. 27 + 29
6. 19 + 54	7. 38 + 43	8. 27 + 18	9. 58 + 18	10. 45 + 23
11. 19 + 15	12. 16 + 37	13. 62 + 35	14. 46 + 34	15. 39 + 26

Using Math

▸ In the first half, the football team scored 18 points. In the second half, they scored 15 points. How many points did they score in all?

They scored _____ points in all.

Work here.

47

Adding 3-Digit Numbers

Step 1 Add the ones.

	hundreds	tens	ones
	2	4	3
+	1	8	2
			5

Step 2 Add the tens.
4 tens + 8 tens = 12 tens
Regroup 12 tens as
1 hundred 2 tens.
Write 2 in the tens' place.
Write 1 in the hundreds' column.

	hundreds	tens	ones
	1		
	2	4	3
+	1	8	2
		2	5

Step 3 Add the hundreds.

	hundreds	tens	ones
	1		
	2	4	3
+	1	8	2
	4	2	5

Guided Practice

▶ Add.

1.	2.	3.	4.	5.
383	463	128	141	279
+126	+265	+356	+290	+420
509				

Practice

▶ Add.

1. 483 + 170	2. 632 + 143	3. 418 + 376	4. 259 + 723	5. 294 + 174
6. 275 + 264	7. 257 + 613	8. 343 + 284	9. 709 + 249	10. 102 + 194
11. 132 + 385	12. 652 + 180	13. 140 + 463	14. 276 + 153	15. 185 + 510

Using Math

▶ Kelly scored 581 points on a computer game.
Then she scored 346 points.
How many points did she score in all?

She scored _____ points in all.

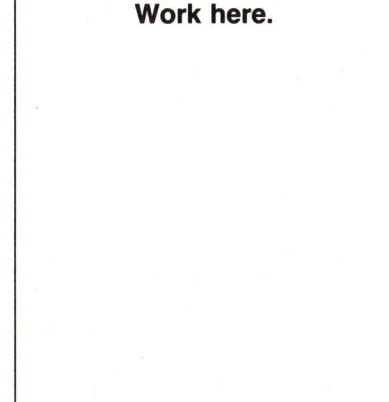

49

Adding 4-Digit Numbers

Step 1 Add the ones.

Step 2 Add the tens.

Step 3 Add the hundreds.
5 hundreds + 8 hundreds
= 13 hundreds
Regroup 13 hundreds as
1 thousand 3 hundreds.
Write 3 in the hundreds' place.
Write 1 in the thousands' column.

thousands	hundreds	tens	ones
1			
2	5	6	1
+ 1	8	1	2
	3	7	3

Step 4 Add the thousands.

thousands	hundreds	tens	ones
1			
2	5	6	1
+ 1	8	1	2
4	3	7	3

Guided Practice

▶ Add.

1.
```
  3,725
+ 1,604
-------
  5,329
```

2.
```
  1,952
+ 1,834
```

3.
```
  2,346
+ 2,231
```

4.
```
  1,242
+ 5,372
```

Practice

Add.

1. $2,613$ $+3,874$	2. $1,623$ $+3,282$	3. $3,405$ $+6,407$	4. $5,532$ $+1,437$
5. $3,714$ $+1,462$	6. $5,746$ $+2,803$	7. $5,732$ $+1,952$	8. $4,185$ $+5,140$
9. $3,129$ $+3,462$	10. $7,624$ $+1,143$	11. $4,928$ $+2,561$	12. $3,640$ $+4,512$
13. $1,842$ $+3,537$	14. $2,853$ $+1,845$	15. $1,025$ $+5,192$	16. $6,035$ $+1,605$

Using Math

One day a jet flew 2,771 miles. The next day it flew 2,527 miles. How many miles did it fly in two days?

It flew _____ miles in two days.

Work here.

Subtracting 2-Digit Numbers

Sometimes you need to **regroup** to subtract.

Step 1 Can you subtract the ones? No.
34 = 3 tens 4 ones
Regroup 3 tens 4 ones as 2 tens 14 ones.
Write 2 in the tens' column.
Write 14 in the ones' column.
Now subtract the ones.

tens	ones
2̸ 3̸	1̸4̸ 4̸
− 1	8
	6

Step 2 Subtract the tens.

tens	ones
2̸ 3̸	1̸4̸ 4̸
− 1	8
1	6

Guided Practice

Subtract.

1. 2 13
   3̸3̸
   − 18
   ―――
   15

2. 61
   − 49

3. 59
   − 26

4. 75
   − 28

5. 32
   − 24

6. 86
   − 27

7. 94
   − 46

8. 43
   − 29

9. 88
   − 42

10. 26
   − 15

Practice

▶ Subtract.

1. 46 − 27	2. 60 − 13	3. 55 − 23	4. 79 − 34	5. 41 − 35
6. 89 − 16	7. 51 − 37	8. 96 − 46	9. 72 − 43	10. 96 − 28
11. 69 − 12	12. 83 − 47	13. 87 − 45	14. 77 − 59	15. 65 − 56

Problem Solving

▶ Make a drawing to solve.

Sam walked 4 blocks to the lake. He walked 3 blocks back toward home to buy ice cream. How many blocks was he from his house?

Answer ____ block.

Subtracting 3-Digit Numbers

Step 1 Subtract the ones.

hundreds	tens	ones
3	5	7
− 1	9	4
		3

Step 2 Can you subtract the tens? No. Then you must regroup. Regroup 3 hundreds 5 tens as 2 hundreds 15 tens. Now subtract the tens.

hundreds	tens	ones
2	15	
3̸	5̸	7
− 1	9	4
	6	3

Step 3 Subtract the hundreds.

hundreds	tens	ones
2	15	
3̸	5̸	7
− 1	9	4
1	6	3

Guided Practice

▶ Subtract.

1.
```
  3 10
  4̸9̸
- 135
  ---
  274
```

2.
```
  938
- 340
```

3.
```
  243
- 125
```

4.
```
  626
- 274
```

5.
```
  917
- 836
```

54

Practice

▸ Subtract.

1. 689 − 493	2. 653 − 341	3. 527 − 242	4. 881 − 232	5. 779 − 241
6. 849 − 154	7. 962 − 239	8. 716 − 156	9. 396 − 257	10. 875 − 591
11. 945 − 180	12. 538 − 186	13. 359 − 286	14. 646 − 536	15. 809 − 317

Using Math

▸ It is 379 miles to camp. The bus has gone 195 miles. How many more miles does it have to go?

It has _____ more miles to go.

Work here.

55

Subtracting 4-Digit Numbers

Step 1 Subtract the ones.

Step 2 Subtract the tens.

Step 3 Can you subtract the hundreds? No. Regroup 3 thousands 2 hundreds as 2 thousands 12 hundreds. Now subtract the hundreds.

Step 4 Subtract the thousands.

thousands	hundreds	tens	ones
2 ~~3~~	12 ~~2~~	5	8
− 1	3	2	6
	9	3	2

thousands	hundreds	tens	ones
2 ~~3~~	12 ~~2~~	5	8
− 1	3	2	6
1	9	3	2

Guided Practice

▷ Subtract.

1.   7 14
      ~~8~~,~~4~~89
    − 3,613
    ─────
      4,876

2.   4,357
    − 1,652

3.   5,747
    − 4,835

4.   3,186
    − 2,062

5.   2,365
    − 1,233

6.   7,742
    − 3,281

7.   8,563
    − 2,429

8.   5,475
    − 2,148

Practice

Subtract.

1. 4,386 − 2,924	2. 9,870 − 6,013	3. 5,864 − 3,174	4. 7,889 − 2,174
5. 9,479 − 2,393	6. 3,425 − 2,501	7. 5,568 − 3,405	8. 5,988 − 2,139
9. 9,146 − 4,615	10. 6,289 − 4,617	11. 6,089 − 2,185	12. 9,397 − 3,580
13. 8,758 − 5,712	14. 3,729 − 1,340	15. 2,075 − 1,610	16. 8,562 − 6,842

Using Math

The school had 3,082 fruit bars in its freezer. When the freezer broke, 1,751 fruit bars melted. How many fruit bars were left?

_____ fruit bars were left.

Work here.

Time to One Hour

A clock tells us the **time**.

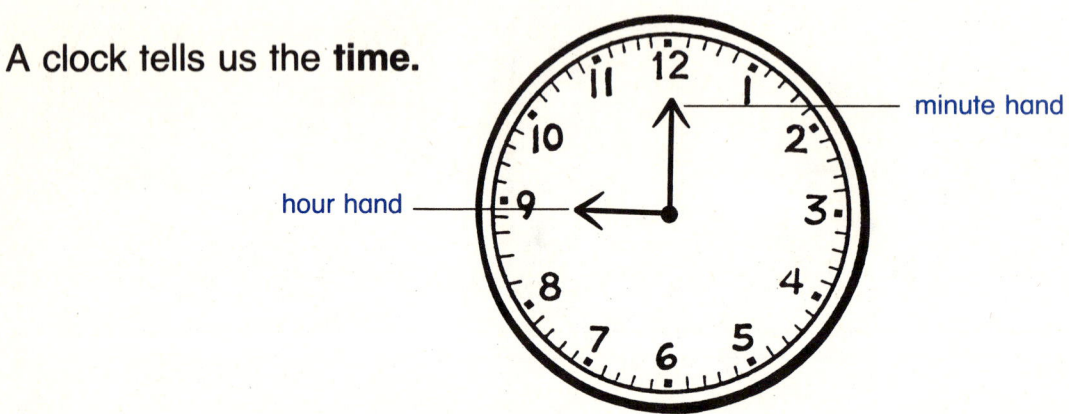

Step 1 Look at the **hour hand.** It is the short hand. It points to 9.

Step 2 Look at the **minute hand.** It is the long hand. It points to 12. When the minute hand points to 12, we say o'clock.

 We say the time is 9 **o'clock.** We write **9:00.**

Guided Practice

▶ Write each time.

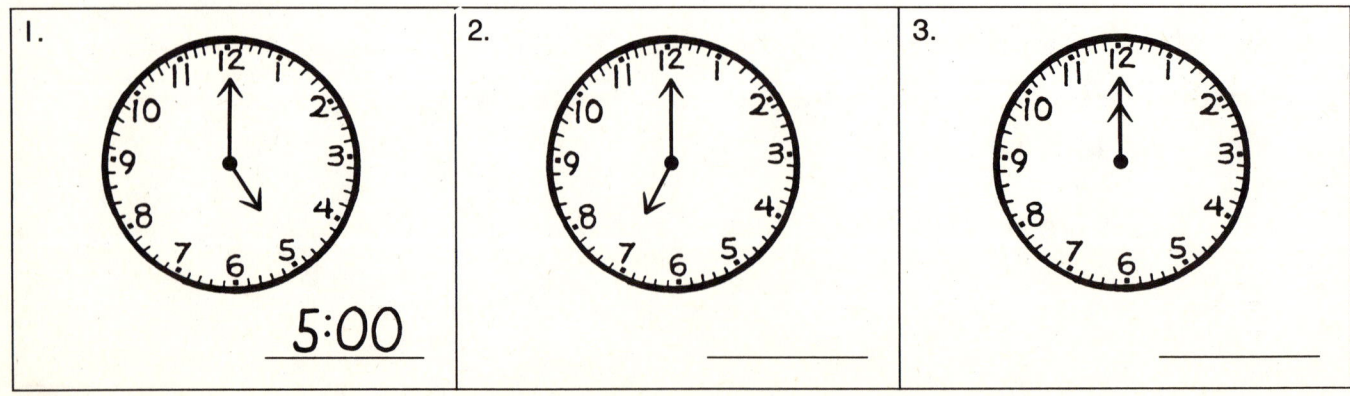

1. 5:00
2. _____
3. _____

Practice

▶ Draw the hands on each clock to show the time.

1. 3:00
2. 6:00
3. 11:00
4. 1:00
5. 2:00
6. 10:00

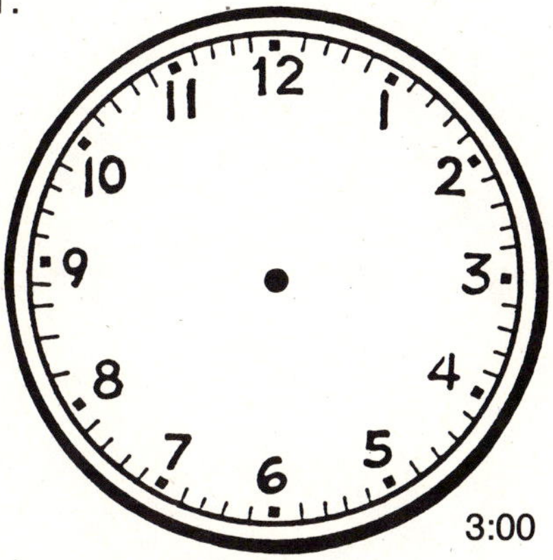

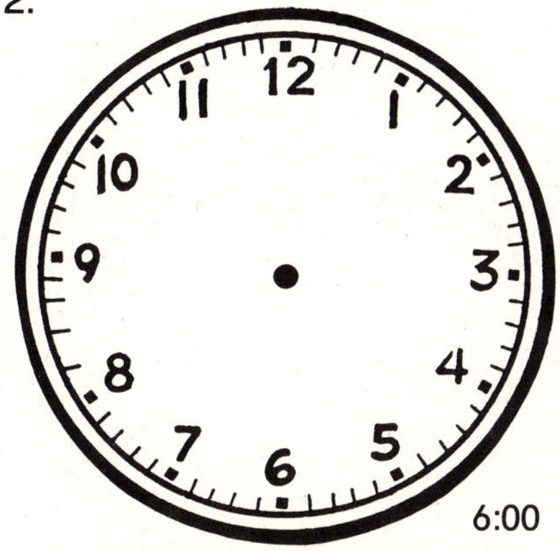

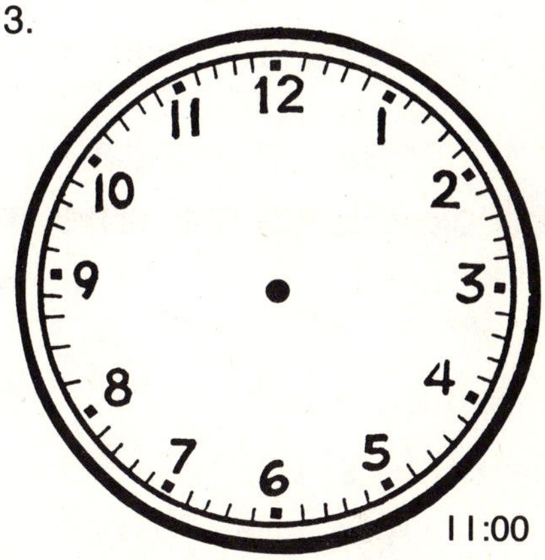

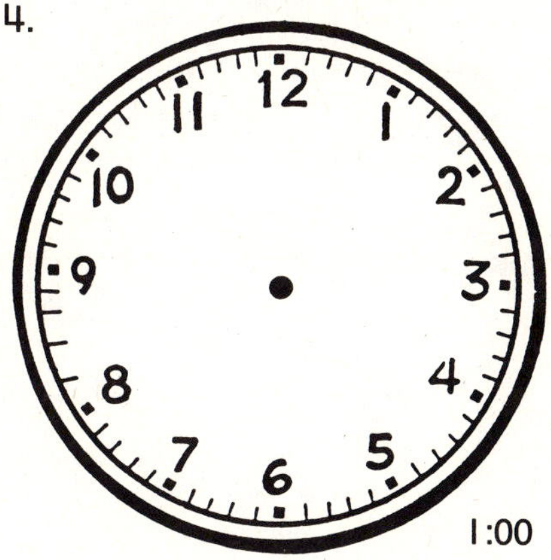

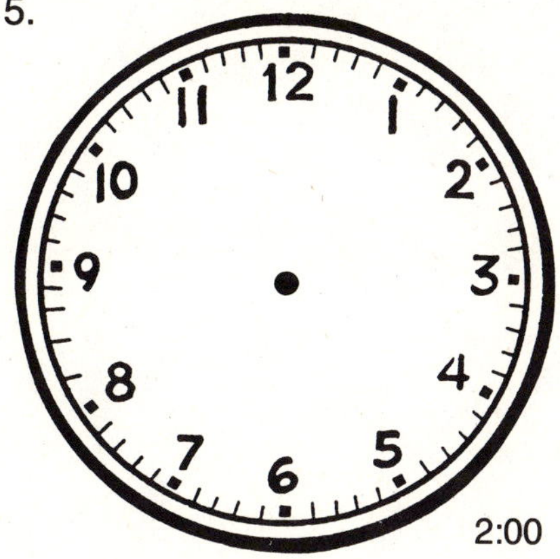

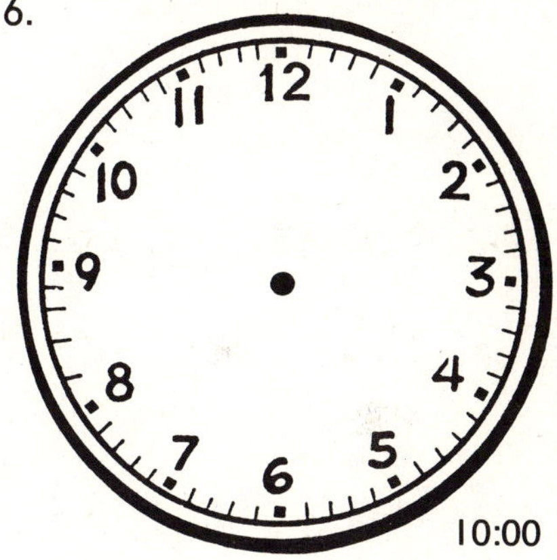

Using Math

▶ School begins at 8:00 in the morning. Draw the hands on the school clock to show the time school begins.

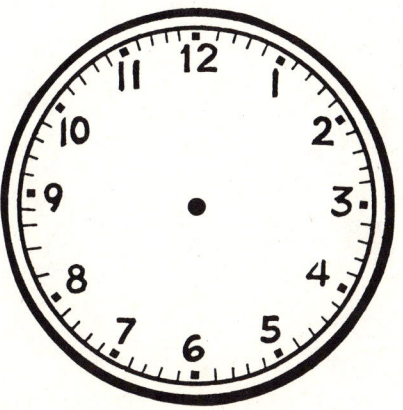

Problem Solving

Use a Table

Sometimes a problem has many facts.
One way to show the facts is to put them in a table.

Mr. Witmer and Ms. Jones asked their classes
to name their favorite kind of books.
The table shows how many students in each class
like each kind of book.

Favorite Kinds of Books

	Fiction	Sports	Science	History
Mr. Witmer's Class	11	8	4	6
Ms. Jones' Class	10	12	5	3

Guided Practice

▶ Use the table to answer.

1. How many students in all like sports books?

    8
    $+12$
    $\overline{20}$ students

2. How many students in all like fiction books?

    $+\underline{}$
     students

3. How many students in all like history books?

    $+\underline{}$
     students

4. How many students in all like science books?

    $+\underline{}$
     students

Practice

Ms. Martin and Mr. Ford took their classes on a hike.
The table shows what each class found.

Things Found on the Hike

	Rocks	Butterflies	Bees	Sticks	Bugs	Flowers
Ms. Martin's Class	35	15	26	44	10	12
Mr. Ford's Class	41	17	18	29	8	13

▸ Use the table to answer.

1. How many butterflies in all were found?

   ___ + ___ butterflies

2. How many flowers in all were found?

   ___ + ___ flowers

3. How many bees in all were found?

   ___ + ___ bees

4. How many bugs in all were found?

   ___ + ___ bugs

5. How many rocks in all were found?

   ___ + ___ rocks

6. How many sticks in all were found?

   ___ + ___ sticks

7. Were more rocks or more sticks found?

   more _____

8. Were more bees or more bugs found?

   more _____

CHAPTER 3 Review

▸ Add.

pages 46–47

1. 38
   +16

2. 17
   +22

3. 34
   +49

4. 69
   +19

5. 19
   +56

6. 52
   +38

7. 42
   +26

8. 15
   +16

pages 48–49

9. 281
   +236

10. 234
   +395

11. 256
   +124

12. 614
   +134

13. 739
   +135

14. 471
   +460

15. 284
   +481

16. 772
   +116

pages 50–51

17. 1,783
   +1,406

18. 5,162
   +1,365

19. 3,763
   +5,712

20. 2,601
   +7,016

21. 6,415
   +2,345

22. 2,423
   +1,870

23. 3,914
   +1,902

24. 4,600
   +2,389

CHAPTER 3 Review

▶ Subtract.

pages 52–53
25. 54
   − 36
	26. 82
	   − 23
		27. 96
		   − 64
			28. 83
			   − 15

pages 54–55
29. 378
   − 183
	30. 496
	   − 219
		31. 816
		   − 452
			32. 645
			   − 532

33. 947
   − 275
	34. 805
	   − 354
		35. 972
		   − 134
			36. 369
			   − 147

pages 56–57
37. 6,298
   − 2,674
	38. 8,179
	   − 6,304
		39. 3,689
		   − 1,593
			40. 7,193
			   − 1,950

▶ Write each time.   pages 58–59

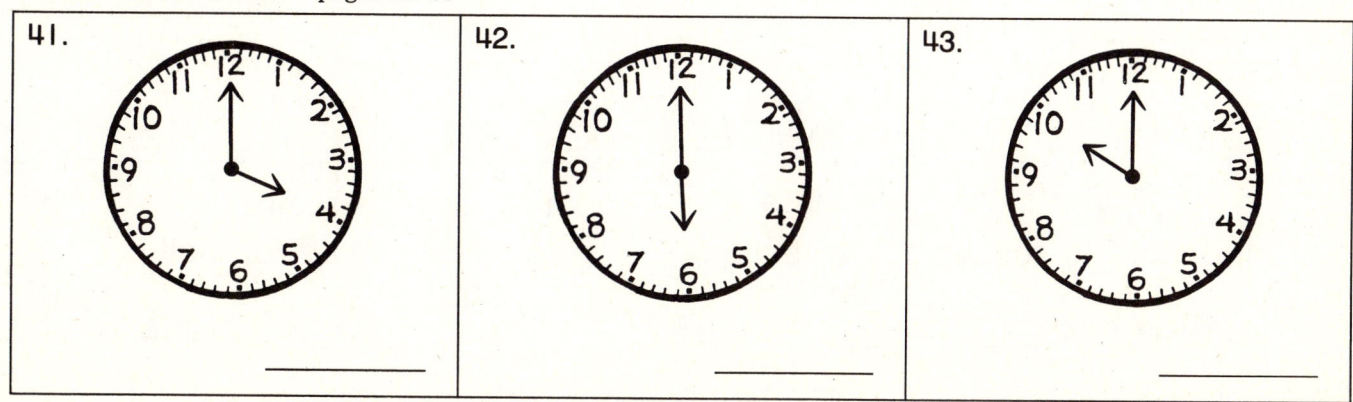

41.   42.   43.

63

CHAPTER 3 Review

Ms. Taylor and Ms. Clark asked their classes which sport they liked. The table shows what students from each class said.

Sports Liked

	Soccer	Football	Baseball	Basketball	Hockey	Tennis
Ms. Taylor's Class	4	6	7	5	2	8
Ms. Clark's Class	3	8	9	6	0	5

▶ Use the table to answer. pages 60–61

44. How many students in all like soccer?

    ___ + ___ students

45. How many students in all like hockey?

    ___ + ___ students

46. How many students in all like baseball?

    ___ + ___ students

47. How many students in all like tennis?

    ___ + ___ students

48. How many students in all like football?

    ___ + ___ students

49. How many students in all like basketball?

    ___ + ___ students

50. In Ms. Taylor's class, do more students like soccer or baseball?

    more like _____

51. Which class has more students who like football?

    _____ class

CHAPTER 3 Test

▶ Add.

1. 28 + 14	2. 35 + 26	3. 19 + 18	4. 61 + 19
5. 635 + 174	6. 271 + 483	7. 293 + 275	8. 3,524 + 1,754

▶ Subtract.

9. 65 − 29	10. 93 − 36	11. 54 − 25	12. 33 − 18
13. 769 − 585	14. 819 − 423	15. 927 − 652	16. 7,387 − 1,423

▶ Write each time.

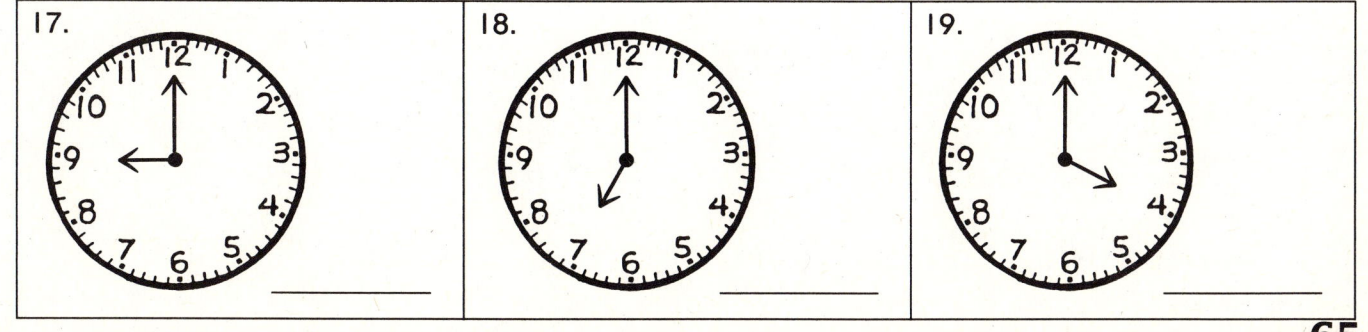

17.   18.   19.

65

CHAPTER 3 — Test

Ben and Eva asked their friends what was their favorite food.
The table shows which foods they liked best.

Favorite Foods

	Pizza	Tacos	Steak	Hot Dogs	Salad	Spaghetti
Ben's Friends	19	7	12	8	11	5
Eva's Friends	10	7	14	13	4	9

▶ Use the table to answer.

20. How many friends in all liked salad?

    +____
    ____ friends

21. How many friends in all liked steak?

    +____
    ____ friends

22. How many friends in all liked pizza?

    +____
    ____ friends

23. How many friends in all liked hot dogs?

    +____
    ____ friends

24. How many friends in all liked spaghetti?

    +____
    ____ friends

25. How many friends in all liked tacos?

    +____
    ____ friends

26. Did more of Eva's friends like steak or hot dogs?

    more liked _____

27. Who had the most friends who liked pizza best?

    _____

CHAPTER 1 Cumulative Review

▸ Add.

pages 2–3

1. 7 + 2
2. 5 + 3
3. 4 + 0
4. 6 + 4
5. 2 + 6
6. 4 + 5
7. 4 + 3
8. 7 + 3

pages 4–5

9. 8 + 3
10. 9 + 5
11. 7 + 6
12. 4 + 8
13. 7 + 7
14. 5 + 7
15. 6 + 5
16. 9 + 4

pages 6–7

17. 8 + 7
18. 9 + 9
19. 7 + 9
20. 9 + 8
21. 8 + 8
22. 9 + 6
23. 8 + 9
24. 9 + 7

67

CHAPTER 1 Cumulative Review

▶ Subtract.

pages 8–9

| 25. 7 − 3 | 26. 10 − 8 | 27. 6 − 4 | 28. 8 − 5 |

pages 10–11

| 29. 11 − 4 | 30. 12 − 8 | 31. 14 − 9 | 32. 13 − 6 |
| 33. 12 − 7 | 34. 11 − 3 | 35. 13 − 8 | 36. 14 − 6 |

pages 12–13

| 37. 18 − 9 | 38. 16 − 8 | 39. 15 − 6 | 40. 17 − 9 |
| 41. 15 − 8 | 42. 17 − 8 | 43. 16 − 9 | 44. 15 − 7 |

▶ Write the day that completes each sentence. pages 14–15

45. The day before Thursday is _____.
                                                  Wednesday   Friday

46. The day after Friday is _____.
                                     Thursday   Saturday

CHAPTER 1 Cumulative Review

▸ **Make a drawing to solve.**
pages 16–17

47. Oscar won 6 ribbons in soccer. He won 6 ribbons in basketball. How many ribbons in all does he have?

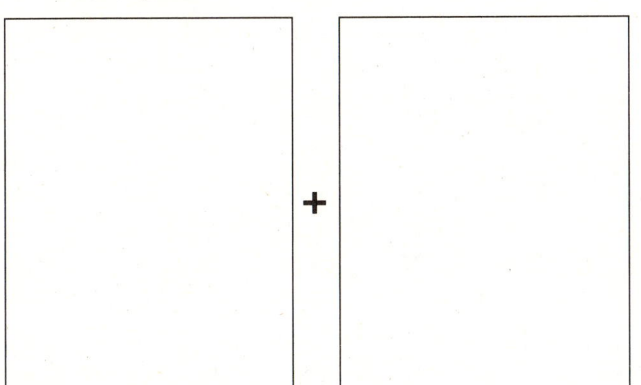

_____ ribbons in all

48. Scott sold 9 vanilla cakes at a bake sale. He sold 3 strawberry cakes, too. How many cakes in all did he sell?

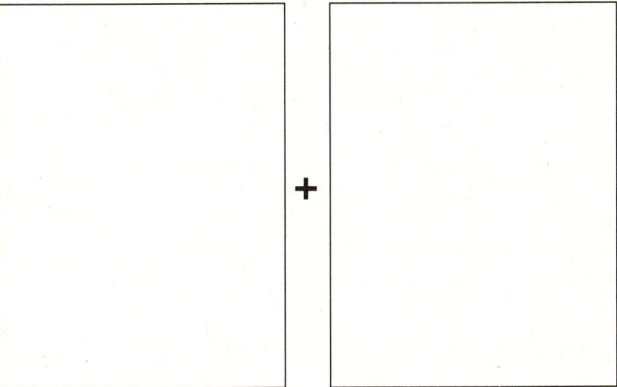

_____ cakes in all

49. Lou had 8 shells in his collection. He found 4 more shells for his collection. How many shells in all did he have then?

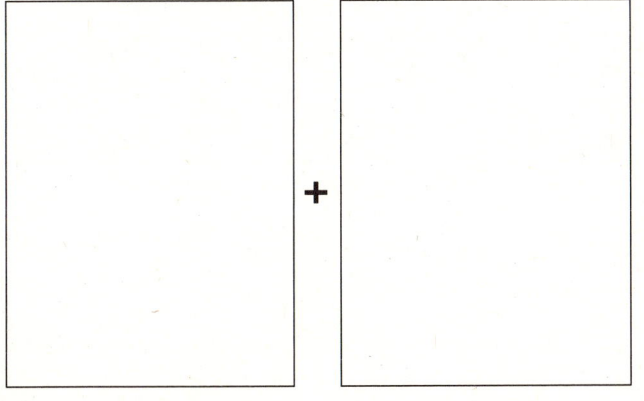

_____ shells in all

50. Marta read 7 books. Gloria read 6 books. How many books in all did they read?

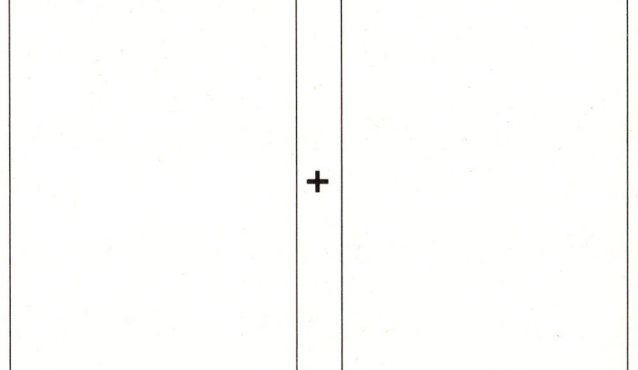

_____ books in all

69

CHAPTER 2 Cumulative Review

▶ Write each number.

pages 24–25

1. 4 tens 6 ones = _____
2. 2 tens 8 ones = _____
3. 9 tens 1 one = _____
4. 6 tens 0 ones = _____
5. 0 tens 3 ones = _____
6. 7 tens 5 ones = _____

pages 26–27

7. 4 hundreds 5 tens 6 ones = _____
8. 9 hundreds 1 ten 7 ones = _____
9. 7 hundreds 0 tens 3 ones = _____
10. 2 hundreds 6 tens 9 ones = _____
11. 8 hundreds 4 tens 5 ones = _____
12. 6 hundreds 8 tens 0 ones = _____

pages 28–29

13. 300 + 40 + 2 = _____
14. 100 + 90 + 7 = _____
15. 500 + 30 + 8 = _____
16. 800 + 8 = _____
17. 700 + 90 = _____
18. 200 + 20 + 3 = _____

pages 30–31

19. 1 thousand 5 hundreds 6 tens 3 ones = _____
20. 6 thousands 0 hundreds 9 tens 1 one = _____
21. 3 thousands 7 hundreds 4 tens 8 ones = _____
22. 7 thousands 2 hundreds 1 ten 0 ones = _____

pages 32–33

23. 1,000 + 400 + 70 + 6 = _____
24. 6,000 + 800 + 5 = _____
25. 3,000 + 100 + 20 + 2 = _____
26. 8,000 + 900 + 80 + 9 = _____
27. 4,000 + 30 + 8 = _____
28. 5,000 + 700 + 6 = _____
29. 2,000 + 500 + 30 = _____
30. 7,000 + 300 + 40 + 2 = _____

CHAPTER 2 Cumulative Review

Compare. Ring > or <.   pages 34–35

31. 47 ⊃> 63	32. 52 ⊃> 33	33. 465 ⊃> 468
34. 113 ⊃> 116	35. 395 ⊃> 387	36. 793 ⊃> 739

Use the September calendar to answer each question.   pages 36–37

September						
Sunday	Monday	Tuesday	Wednesday	Thursday	Friday	Saturday
		1	2	3	4	5
6	7	8	9	10	11	12
13	14	15	16	17	18	19
20	21	22	23	24	25	26
27	28	29	30			

37. How many days are there in September? _____

38. On what day does September begin? _____

39. How many Thursdays are there in September? _____

40. What is the date after September 14? _____

41. What day of the week is September 4? _____

42. What is the date of the first Wednesday? _____

71

CHAPTER 2 Cumulative Review

Make a drawing to solve.
pages 38–39

43. Rodney walked 4 blocks to the store.
    He walked 3 more blocks to Rob's house.
    How many blocks in all did he walk?

    Answer _____ blocks.

44. Aldo lives 9 blocks from the school.
    He walks past Karen's house on his way to school.
    Karen lives 6 blocks from the school.
    How many blocks apart do Aldo and Karen live?

    Answer _____ blocks.

45. Sue rode her bike 8 blocks from home to Beth's house.
    She rode 6 blocks back toward home to the bowling alley.
    How far is the bowling alley from Sue's house?

    Answer _____ blocks.

46. Donna walked 7 blocks to Terry's house.
    She walked 4 more blocks to Guy's house.
    How many blocks in all did she walk?

    Answer _____ blocks.

CHAPTER 3 Cumulative Review

▶ Add.

pages 46–47			
1. 16 + 29	2. 37 + 56	3. 78 + 12	4. 52 + 29
pages 48–51			
5. 253 + 162	6. 364 + 208	7. 191 + 141	8. 3,682 + 2,411

▶ Subtract.

pages 52–53			
9. 46 − 19	10. 53 − 27	11. 34 − 16	12. 87 − 69
pages 54–57			
13. 867 − 671	14. 653 − 472	15. 789 − 199	16. 6,416 − 2,235

▶ Write each time.   pages 58–59

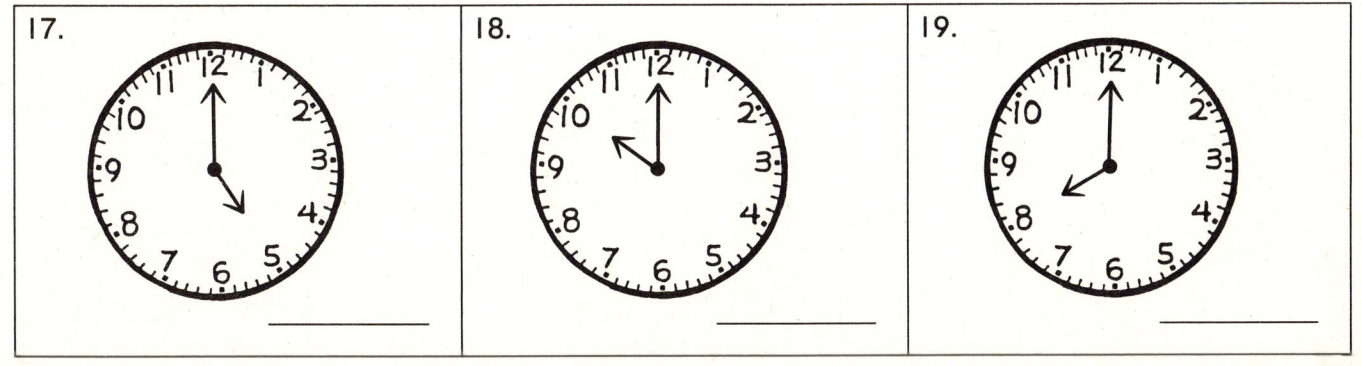

17.   18.   19.

73

CHAPTER 3 Cumulative Review

Chad counted the shirt colors of the students on the playground. The table shows what he found.

Shirt Colors

	Red	Green	Yellow	Blue	Orange	Purple
Boys	24	10	16	33	0	4
Girls	18	12	5	29	3	21

▶ Use the table to answer. pages 60–61

20. How many students were wearing yellow shirts?
 	
      +
   _____
         students
	21. How many students were wearing orange shirts?
	
	      +
	   _____
	         students

22. How many students were wearing red shirts?
 	
      +
   _____
         students
	23. How many students were wearing purple shirts?
	
	      +
	   _____
	         students

24. How many students were wearing green shirts?
 	
      +
   _____
         students
	25. How many students were wearing blue shirts?
	
	      +
	   _____
	         students

26. Did the boys wear more blue shirts or more red shirts? more _____ shirts	27. Did more girls or more boys wear green shirts? more _____

74

CHAPTER 4
Multiplication Facts Through 5

There are 3 cars on the roller coaster. Each car carries 4 people. How many people in all can the roller coaster carry?

Solve

▶ Write a problem about a carnival ride that you like.

Multiplying by 2

You can add to find how many in all.

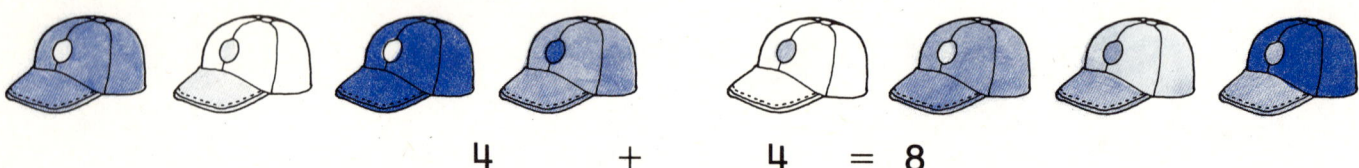

4 + 4 = 8

When the groups are equal, you can also **multiply** to find how many in all. How many caps are there in all?

Step 1 Count the number in each group: 4.

Step 2 Count the groups: 2.

Step 3 Write: 2 × 4 = 8   or $\begin{array}{r} 4 \\ \times\, 2 \\ \hline 8 \end{array}$

Step 4 Say: There are 8 caps in all.

Guided Practice

▷ Multiply.

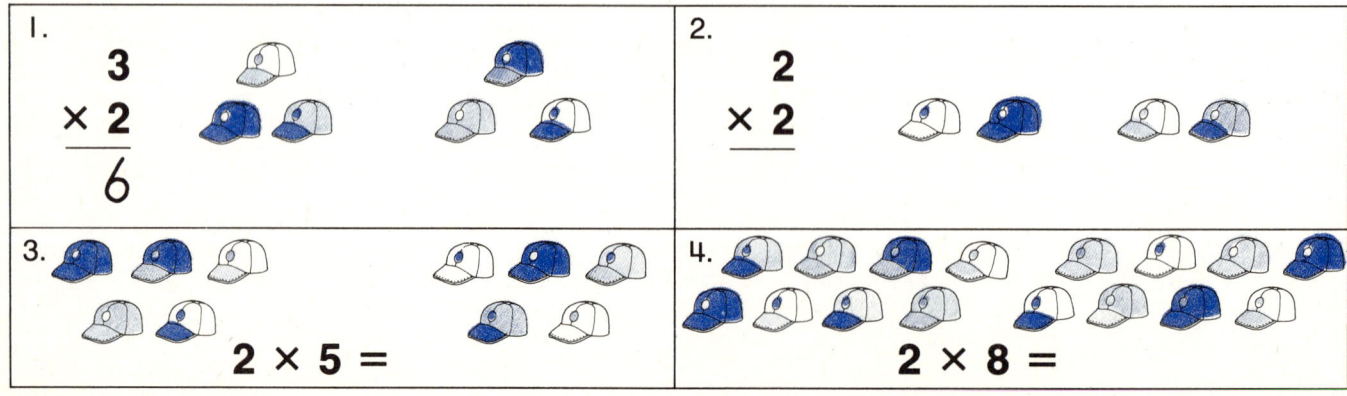

1. $\begin{array}{r} 3 \\ \times\, 2 \\ \hline 6 \end{array}$

2. $\begin{array}{r} 2 \\ \times\, 2 \\ \hline \end{array}$

3. 2 × 5 =

4. 2 × 8 =

76

Practice

Multiply.

1. $\begin{array}{r}6\\ \times 2\\ \hline\end{array}$	2. $\begin{array}{r}9\\ \times 2\\ \hline\end{array}$

3. $\begin{array}{r}7\\ \times 2\\ \hline\end{array}$	4. $\begin{array}{r}2\\ \times 2\\ \hline\end{array}$	5. $\begin{array}{r}1\\ \times 2\\ \hline\end{array}$	6. $\begin{array}{r}8\\ \times 2\\ \hline\end{array}$
7. $\begin{array}{r}9\\ \times 2\\ \hline\end{array}$	8. $\begin{array}{r}7\\ \times 2\\ \hline\end{array}$	9. $\begin{array}{r}5\\ \times 2\\ \hline\end{array}$	10. $\begin{array}{r}6\\ \times 2\\ \hline\end{array}$
11. $2 \times 4 =$	12. $2 \times 1 =$	13. $2 \times 3 =$	14. $2 \times 2 =$

Problem Solving

Use the table to answer.
Ms. Cruz and Ms. Parks made a table to show the kind of shoes their students wear to school. Which class wears more gym shoes?

_____ class

Shoes	Gym Shoes	Other Shoes
Ms. Cruz's Class	19	12
Ms. Parks' Class	24	8

2 Multiplying by 3

  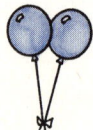

How many balloons are there in all?

Step 1 Count the number in each group: 2.

Step 2 Count the groups: 3.

Step 3 Write: 3 × 2 = 6 or $\begin{array}{r} 2 \\ \times\,3 \\ \hline 6 \end{array}$

Step 4 Say: There are 6 balloons in all.

The numbers we multiply are called **factors**. 3 and 2 are factors. The answer is called the **product**. 6 is the product.

Guided Practice

▸ Multiply.

1. $\begin{array}{r} 3 \\ \times\,3 \\ \hline 9 \end{array}$

2. $\begin{array}{r} 1 \\ \times\,3 \\ \hline \end{array}$

3. 3 × 4 =

4. 3 × 5 =

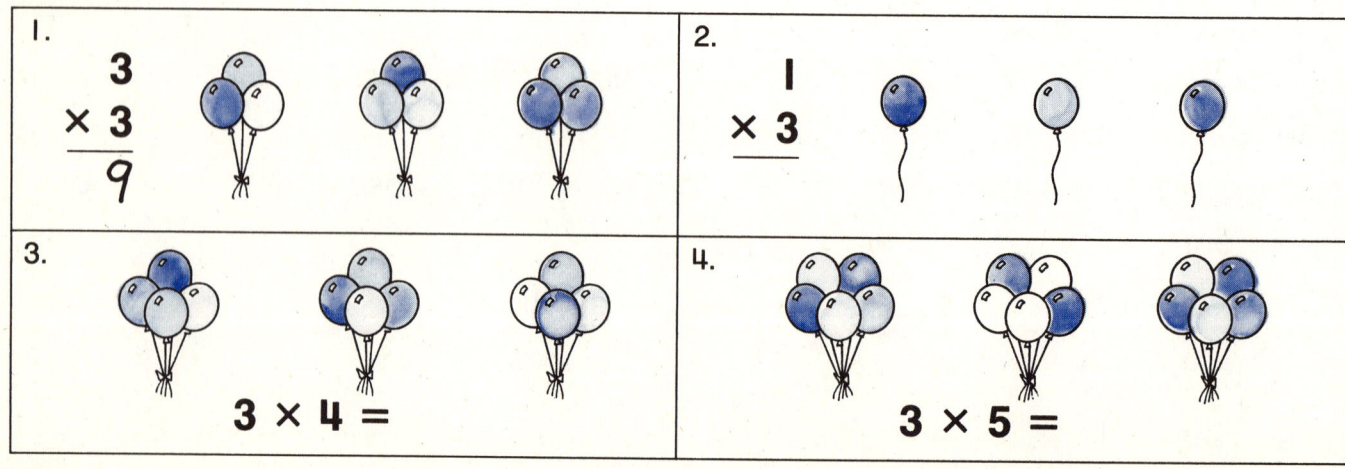

78

Practice

▸ Multiply.

1. $\begin{array}{r}7\\\times 3\\\hline\end{array}$		2. $\begin{array}{r}6\\\times 3\\\hline\end{array}$
3. $\begin{array}{r}8\\\times 3\\\hline\end{array}$	4. $\begin{array}{r}9\\\times 3\\\hline\end{array}$	5. $\begin{array}{r}4\\\times 3\\\hline\end{array}$ 6. $\begin{array}{r}5\\\times 3\\\hline\end{array}$
7. $\begin{array}{r}3\\\times 3\\\hline\end{array}$	8. $\begin{array}{r}6\\\times 3\\\hline\end{array}$	9. $\begin{array}{r}8\\\times 3\\\hline\end{array}$ 10. $\begin{array}{r}1\\\times 3\\\hline\end{array}$
11. $3 \times 9 =$	12. $3 \times 3 =$	13. $3 \times 2 =$ 14. $3 \times 7 =$

Using Math

▸ The science fair has 3 tables with 4 projects set up on each table. How many projects are there in all?

There are _____ projects in all.

Work here.

Multiplying by 4

How many brushes are there in all?

Step 1 Count the number in each group: 3.

Step 2 Count the groups: 4.

Step 3 Write: 4 × 3 = 12   or $\begin{array}{r}3\\\times 4\\\hline 12\end{array}$

Step 4 Say: There are 12 brushes in all.

> The order of the factors does **not** change the product.

Guided Practice

▶ Multiply.

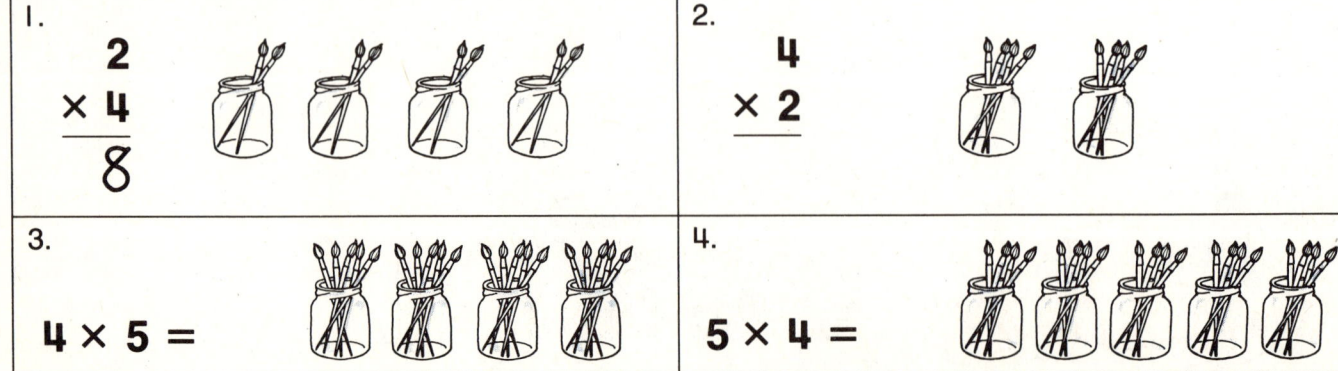

Practice

Multiply.

1. $\begin{array}{r}6\\ \times 4\\ \hline\end{array}$			2. $\begin{array}{r}4\\ \times 6\\ \hline\end{array}$	
3. $\begin{array}{r}1\\ \times 4\\ \hline\end{array}$	4. $\begin{array}{r}4\\ \times 1\\ \hline\end{array}$	5. $\begin{array}{r}9\\ \times 4\\ \hline\end{array}$	6. $\begin{array}{r}4\\ \times 9\\ \hline\end{array}$	
7. $\begin{array}{r}8\\ \times 4\\ \hline\end{array}$	8. $\begin{array}{r}4\\ \times 8\\ \hline\end{array}$	9. $\begin{array}{r}4\\ \times 4\\ \hline\end{array}$	10. $\begin{array}{r}7\\ \times 4\\ \hline\end{array}$	
11. $4 \times 7 =$	12. $4 \times 1 =$	13. $4 \times 6 =$	14. $4 \times 4 =$	

Using Math

There are 4 students studying space. Each student made 2 posters. How many posters are there in all?

There are ____ posters in all.

Work here.

Multiplying by 5

How many petals are there in all?

Step 1 Count the number (petals) in each group: 6.

Step 2 Count the groups: 5.

Step 3 Write: 5 × 6 = 30   or $\begin{array}{r} 6 \\ \times\, 5 \\ \hline 30 \end{array}$

Step 4 Say: There are 30 petals in all.

Guided Practice

▸ Multiply.

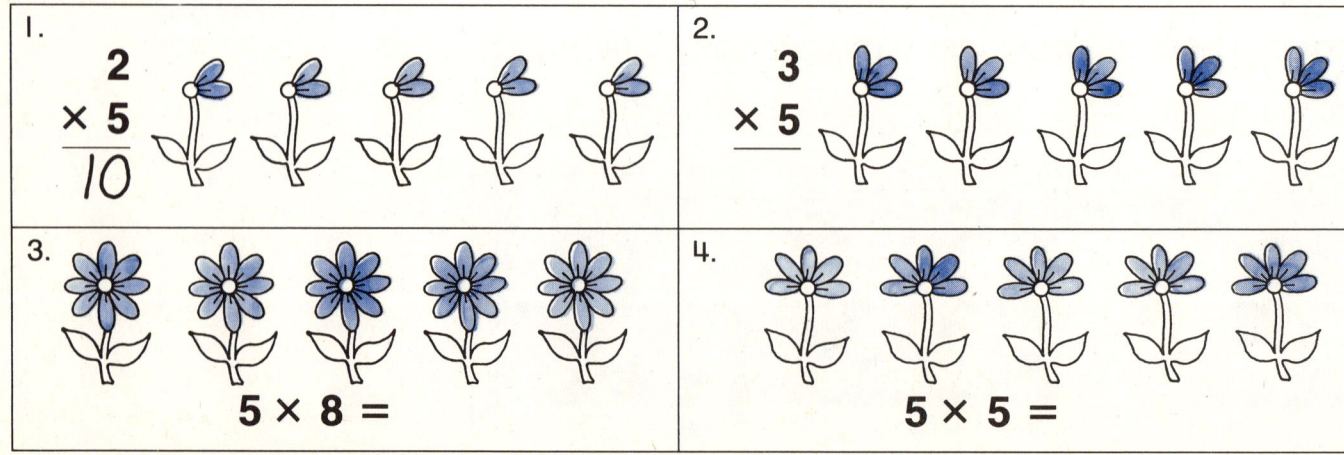

Practice

▶ Multiply.

1. $\begin{array}{r} 7 \\ \times 5 \\ \hline \end{array}$	2. $\begin{array}{r} 4 \\ \times 5 \\ \hline \end{array}$

3. $\begin{array}{r} 1 \\ \times 5 \\ \hline \end{array}$	4. $\begin{array}{r} 9 \\ \times 5 \\ \hline \end{array}$	5. $\begin{array}{r} 8 \\ \times 5 \\ \hline \end{array}$	6. $\begin{array}{r} 5 \\ \times 3 \\ \hline \end{array}$
7. $\begin{array}{r} 5 \\ \times 5 \\ \hline \end{array}$	8. $\begin{array}{r} 5 \\ \times 2 \\ \hline \end{array}$	9. $\begin{array}{r} 5 \\ \times 7 \\ \hline \end{array}$	10. $\begin{array}{r} 5 \\ \times 1 \\ \hline \end{array}$
11. $5 \times 3 =$	12. $4 \times 5 =$	13. $5 \times 2 =$	14. $5 \times 6 =$

Using Math

▶ There are 5 rows of students in the marching band. There are 9 students in each row. How many students are there in all?

There are _____ students in all.

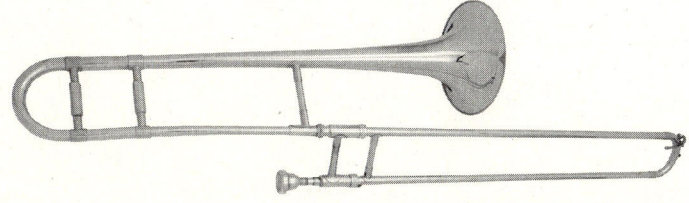

Work here.

83

Multiplying by 0 and 1

How many tents are there in all?

Step 1 Count the number in each group: 3.

Step 2 Count the groups: 1.

Step 3 Write: 1 × 3 = 3   or $\begin{array}{r} 3 \\ \times\, 1 \\ \hline 3 \end{array}$

Step 4 Say: There are 3 tents in all.

> 1 × any number = the same number
>
> 0 × any number = 0

Guided Practice

▶ Multiply.

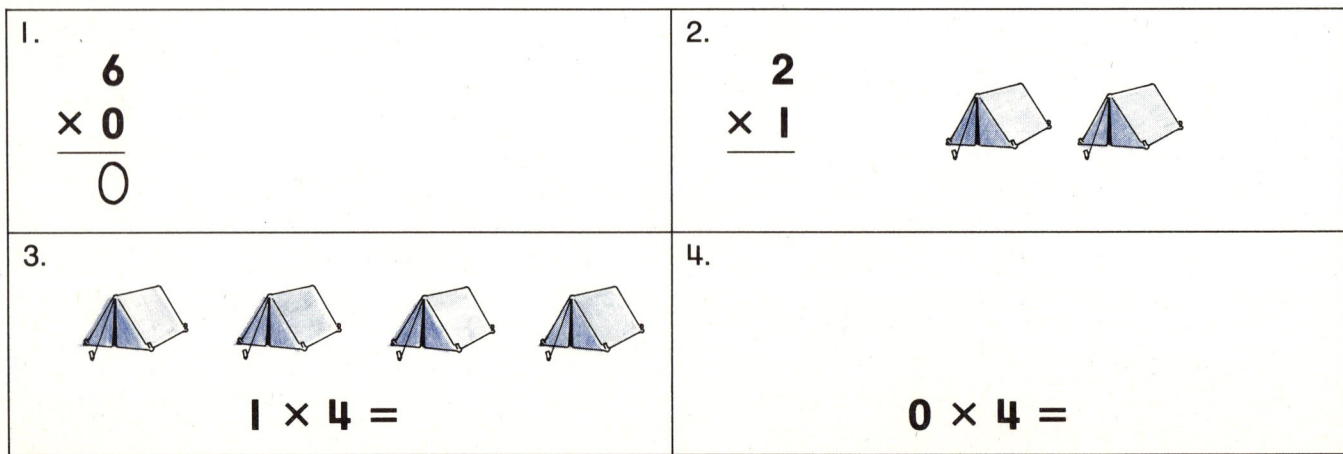

1. $\begin{array}{r} 6 \\ \times\, 0 \\ \hline 0 \end{array}$

2. $\begin{array}{r} 2 \\ \times\, 1 \\ \hline \end{array}$

3. 1 × 4 =

4. 0 × 4 =

Practice

▸ Multiply.

1. 9 × 0	2. 1 × 1
3. 8 × 0	4. 6 × 1	5. 1 × 1	6. 3 × 0
7. 7 × 1	8. 5 × 0	9. 0 × 0	10. 9 × 1
11. 0 × 6 =	12. 1 × 8 =	13. 0 × 7 =	14. 1 × 3 =

Using Math

▸ Juan went to camp for one week. How many days was Juan at camp?

Juan was at camp _____ days.

Work here.

Multiplication Table 0–5

A **multiplication table** can help you find the product of two factors.

×	0	1	2	3	4	5
0	0	0	0	0	0	0
1	0	1	2	3	4	5
2	0	2	4	6	8	10
3	0	3	6	9	12	15
4	0	4	8	12	16	20
5	0	5	10	15	20	25

This is how you use the table to find the product of 2 × 4.

Step 1 Find the first factor in the column under the ×.

Step 2 Move to the right until you are under the second factor.

Step 3 Read the product: 8.

Guided Practice

▶ Find each product using the multiplication table above.

1. 1 × 3 = 3	2. 4 × 5 =	3. 2 × 0 =
4. 5 × 2 =	5. 3 × 4 =	6. 2 × 2 =

Practice

▷ Multiply. You may use the multiplication table.

1. $5 \times 5 =$	2. $4 \times 4 =$	3. $2 \times 3 =$
4. $3 \times 2 =$	5. $3 \times 3 =$	6. $2 \times 5 =$
7. $2 \times 1 =$	8. $4 \times 2 =$	9. $0 \times 0 =$
10. $1 \times 4 =$	11. $5 \times 4 =$	12. $4 \times 3 =$
13. $0 \times 3 =$	14. $4 \times 1 =$	15. $1 \times 5 =$
16. $1 \times 1 =$	17. $3 \times 5 =$	18. $4 \times 0 =$

Using Math

▷ In art class, 5 students made clay pots.
Each student made 3 clay pots.
How many clay pots were made in all?

_____ clay pots were made in all.

Time to the Half Hour

What time is it?

Step 1 Look at the hour hand. It is between 2 and 3. When the hour hand is between two numbers, the smaller number tells the hour. The hour is 2.

Step 2 Look at the minute hand. It points to 6. When the minute hand points to 6, we say **thirty.** We write 30.

The time is 2:30.

Guided Practice

▶ Write each time.

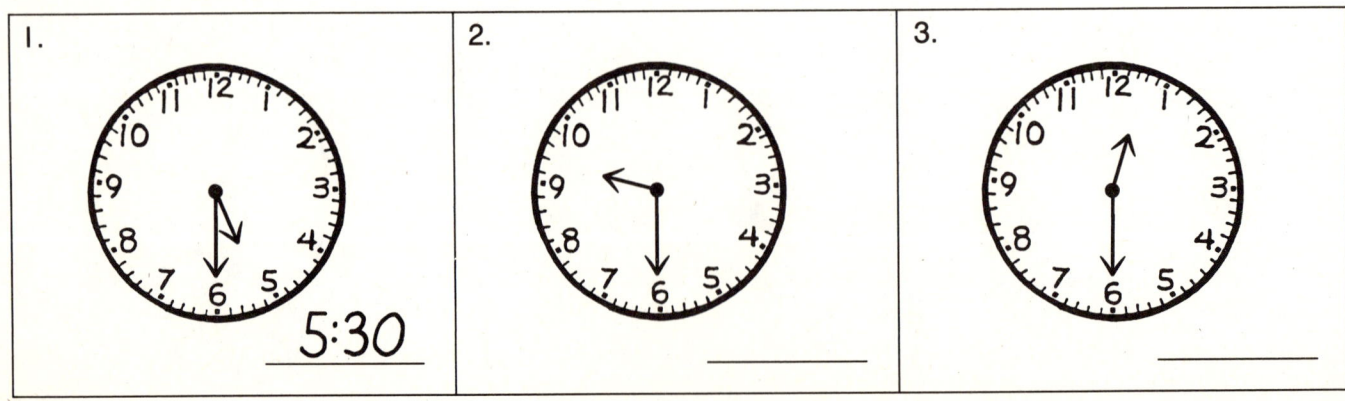

Practice

▶ Draw the hands on each clock to show the time.

1. 3:30	2. 7:00	3. 10:30
4. 6:30	5. 11:30	6. 1:30

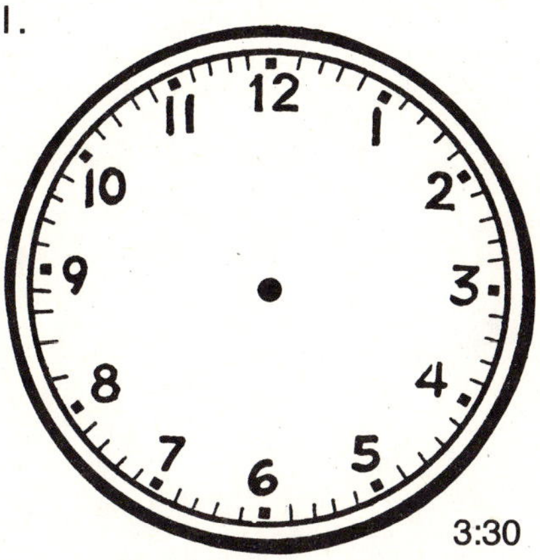

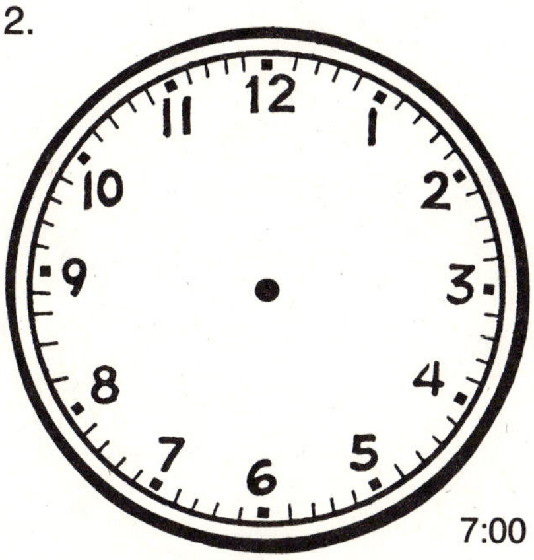

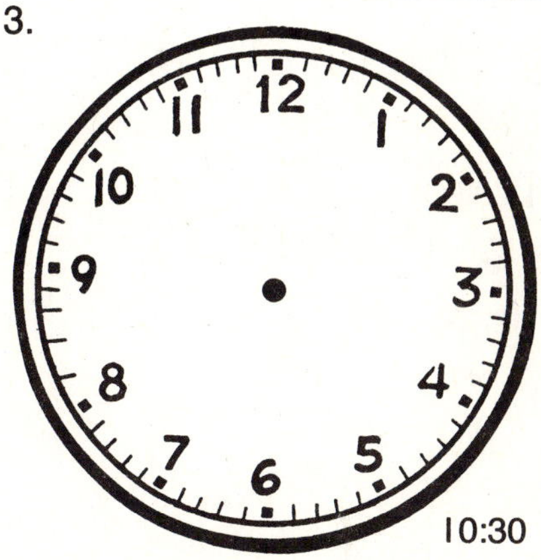

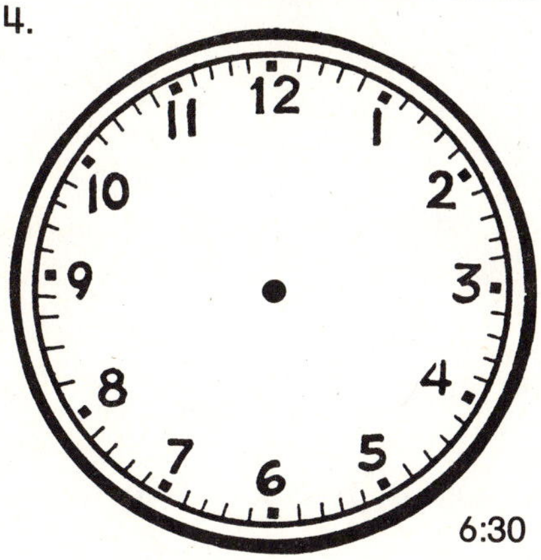

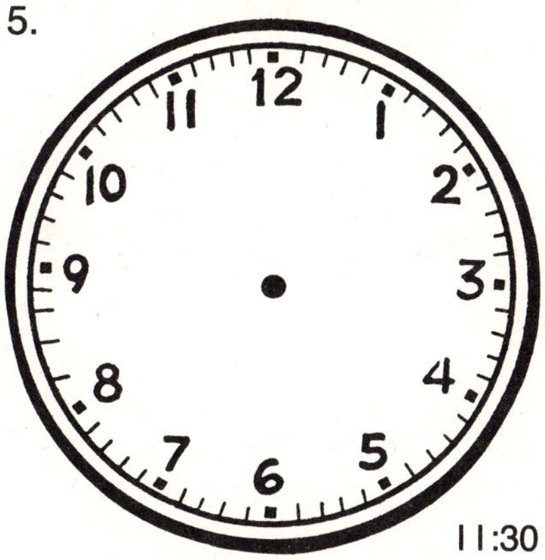

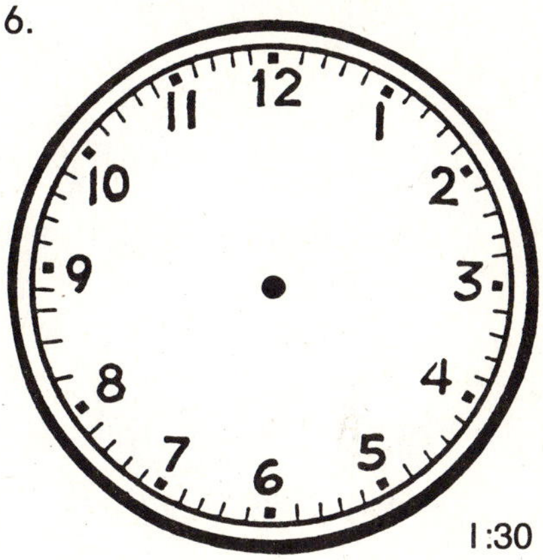

Using Math

▶ Look at Lisa's morning class schedule. Draw hands on the clock to show what time she has math.

Schedule
- Math 8:30
- Reading 9:30
- Art 10:30
- Lunch 11:30

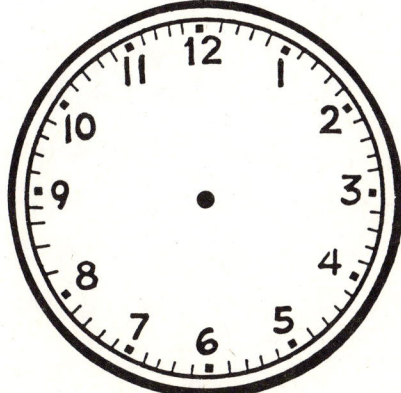

89

8 Problem Solving

Make a Table

Bill went to the store to buy some marbles.
One marble cost 3¢.
Bill made a table to show how much 2, 3, and 4 marbles will cost.

Marble Prices

Marbles	1	2	3	4
Cost	3¢	6¢	9¢	12¢

How did Bill find the price of 2 marbles?
He multiplied the price of one marble, 3¢, times 2 marbles.

```
   3¢
 x 2 marbles
   ¢
```

How did Bill find the price of 3 marbles?
He multiplied 3¢ times 3 marbles.
Write 9¢ in the table.

```
   3¢
 x 3 marbles
   ¢
```

How did Bill find the price of 4 marbles?
He multiplied 3¢ times 4 marbles.
Write 12¢ in the table.

```
   3¢
 x 4 marbles
   ¢
```

Guided Practice

▶ Write numbers to make the table.

1. One pencil costs 5¢. How much is it for 2, 3, and 4 pencils?

Pencil Prices

Pencils	1	2	3	4
Cost	5¢	10¢	¢	¢

Practice

▶ Write numbers to make the tables.

1. Beth bought a piece of candy for 2¢.
   How much will 2, 3, and 4 pieces of candy cost?

Candy Prices

Candy	1	2	3	4
Cost	**2¢**	___¢	___¢	___¢

2. Joe bought some peanuts for 1¢ each.
   How much did he pay for 2, 3, and 4 peanuts?

Peanut Prices

Peanuts	1	2	3	4
Cost	**1¢**	___¢	___¢	___¢

3. Carmen paid 4¢ for a walnut.
   How much will 2, 3, and 4 walnuts cost?

Walnut Prices

Walnuts	1	2	3	4
Cost	**4¢**	___¢	___¢	___¢

4. Lisa bought a gumball for 3¢.
   How much will 2, 3, and 4 gumballs cost?

Gumball Prices

Gumballs	1	2	3	4
Cost	**3¢**	___¢	___¢	___¢

5. Tim bought a grape for 5¢.
   How much will 2, 3, 4, and 5 grapes cost?

Grape Prices

Grapes	1	2	3	4	5
Cost	**5¢**	___¢	___¢	___¢	___¢

CHAPTER 4 Review

▶ Multiply.

pages 76–77			
1. 5 × 2	2. 7 × 2	3. 3 × 2	4. 6 × 2
5. 2 × 2	6. 4 × 2	7. 1 × 2	8. 9 × 2
pages 78–79 9. 8 × 3	10. 0 × 3	11. 6 × 3	12. 5 × 3
pages 80–81 13. 3 × 4	14. 7 × 4	15. 4 × 4	16. 9 × 4
pages 82–83 17. 9 × 5	18. 3 × 5	19. 6 × 5	20. 4 × 5
21. 5 × 5	22. 8 × 5	23. 0 × 5	24. 7 × 5

CHAPTER 4 Review

▶ **Multiply.** pages 84–85

25. 7 × 0	26. 1 × 1	27. 4 × 0	28. 0 × 1
29. 8 × 1	30. 0 × 0	31. 9 × 1	32. 6 × 0

▶ **Draw the hands on each clock to show the time.** pages 88–89

33. 2:30

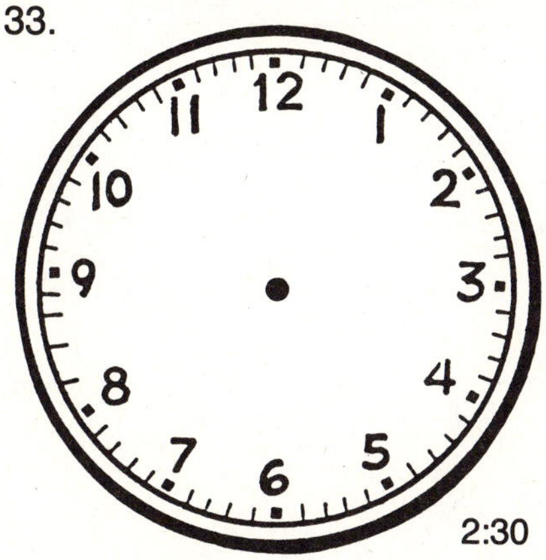

34. 11:30

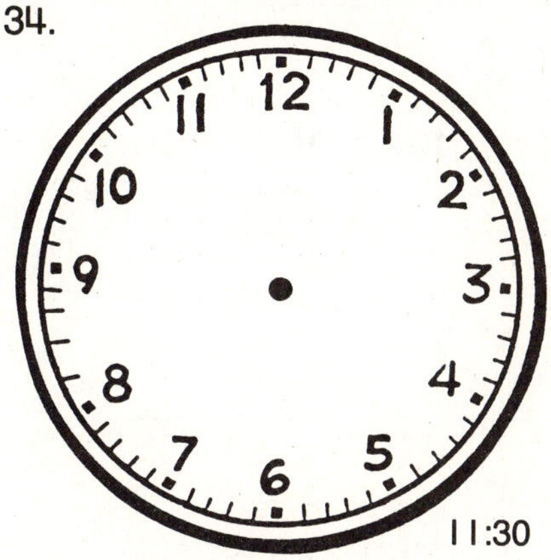

35. 3:30

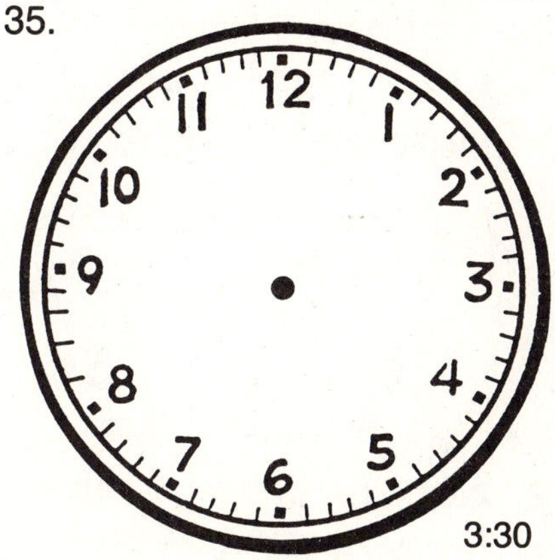

36. 4:30

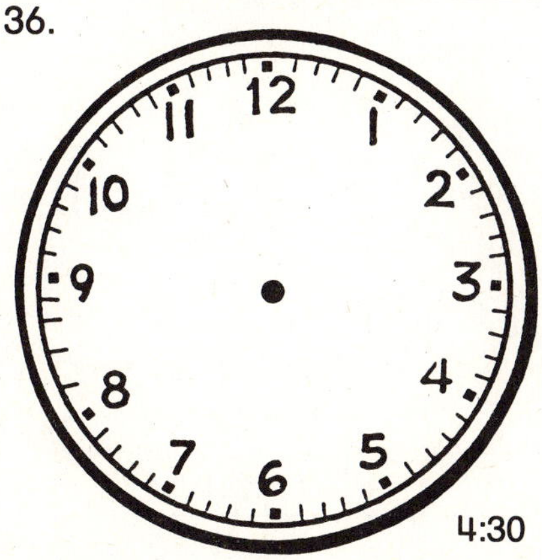

37. 8:30

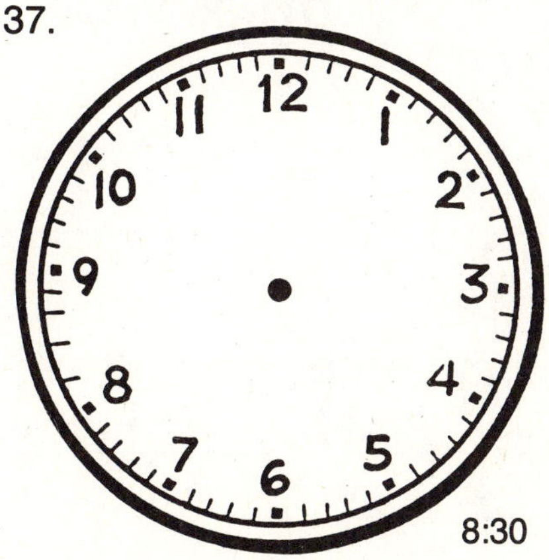

38. 12:30

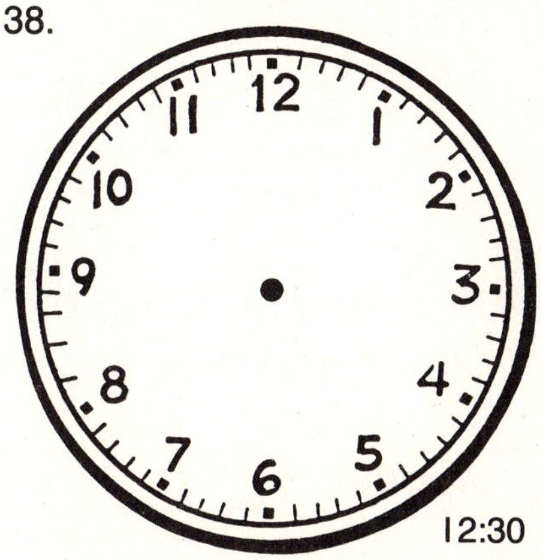

93

CHAPTER 4 Review

▶ Write numbers to make the tables.
pages 90–91

39. Tina bought a mint for 1¢.
    How much will 2, 3, and 4 mints cost?

Mint Prices

Mints	1	2	3	4
Cost	1¢	___¢	___¢	___¢

40. John paid 3¢ for a cookie.
    How much will 2, 3, and 4 cookies cost?

Cookie Prices

Cookies	1	2	3	4
Cost	3¢	___¢	___¢	___¢

41. Isa bought a bag of popcorn for 5¢.
    How much will 2, 3, and 4 bags of popcorn cost?

Popcorn Prices

Popcorn	1 Bag	2 Bags	3 Bags	4 Bags
Cost	5¢	___¢	___¢	___¢

42. Sam bought a drink for 6¢.
    How much will 2, 3, and 4 drinks cost?

Drink Prices

Drinks	1	2	3	4
Cost	6¢	___¢	___¢	___¢

43. Gail bought an apple for 10¢.
    How much will 2, 3, 4, and 5 apples cost?

Apple Prices

Apples	1	2	3	4	5
Cost	10¢	___¢	___¢	___¢	___¢

CHAPTER 4 Test

▶ Multiply.

1. 9 × 2	2. 4 × 3	3. 8 × 2	4. 7 × 3
5. 8 × 4	6. 2 × 4	7. 9 × 4	8. 6 × 4
9. 7 × 5	10. 4 × 5	11. 2 × 5	12. 9 × 5
13. 6 × 1	14. 2 × 0	15. 5 × 1	16. 8 × 0

▶ Draw the hands on each clock to show the time.

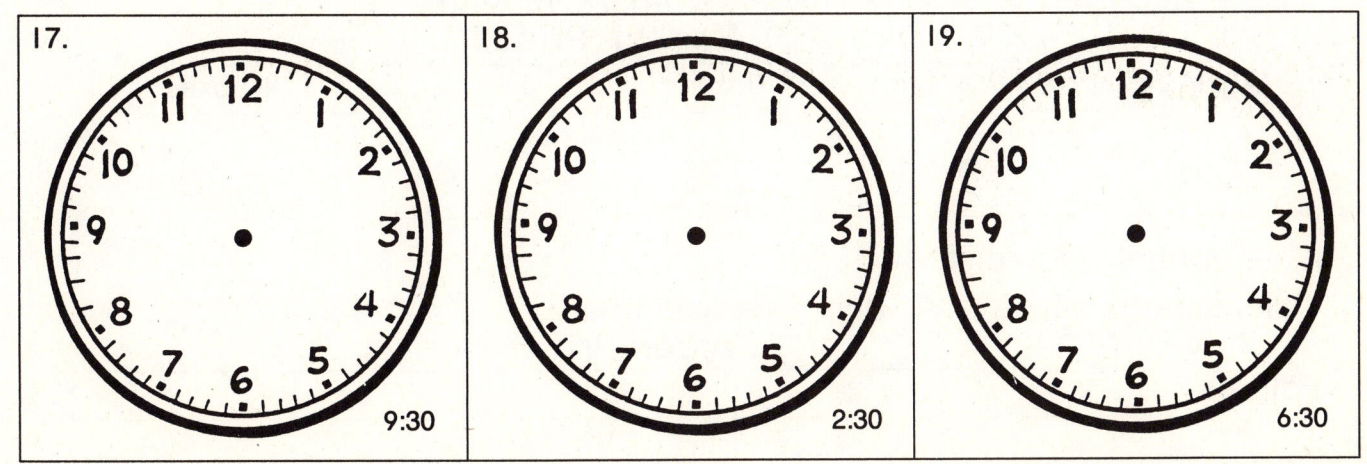

17. 9:30   18. 2:30   19. 6:30

95

Test

▸ Write numbers to make the tables.

20. Pete bought a pencil for 2¢.
    How much will 2, 3, and 4 pencils cost?

    Pencil Prices

Pencils	1	2	3	4
Cost	2¢	___¢	___¢	___¢

21. Sara paid 4¢ for a pen.
    How much will 2, 3, and 4 pens cost?

    Pen Prices

Pens	1	2	3	4
Cost	4¢	___¢	___¢	___¢

22. Cathy paid 7¢ for a pad of paper.
    How much will 2, 3, and 4 pads of paper cost?

    Paper Prices

Paper	1 Pad	2 Pads	3 Pads	4 Pads
Cost	7¢	___¢	___¢	___¢

23. Cody bought a box of markers for 6¢.
    How much will 2, 3, and 4 boxes of markers cost?

    Marker Prices

Markers	1 Box	2 Boxes	3 Boxes	4 Boxes
Cost	6¢	___¢	___¢	___¢

24. Jill bought a folder for 10¢.
    How much will 2, 3, 4, and 5 folders cost?

    Folder Prices

Folders	1	2	3	4	5
Cost	10¢	___¢	___¢	___¢	___¢

CHAPTER 5
Multiplication Facts Through 9

Dawna and Diana collect shells. They place their shells in rows. There are 7 rows. There are 5 shells in each row. How many shells are there in all?

Solve

▶ Write a problem about a collection that you would like.

Multiplying by 6

You know that you can multiply to find how many in all.

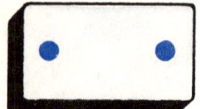  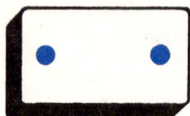  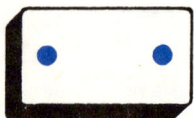 

How many dots are there in all?

Step 1 Count the number in each group: 2.

Step 2 Count the groups: 6.

Step 3 Write: 6 × 2 = 12   or $\begin{array}{r} 2 \\ \times\,6 \\ \hline 12 \end{array}$

Step 4 Say: There are 12 dots in all.

Guided Practice

▶ Multiply.

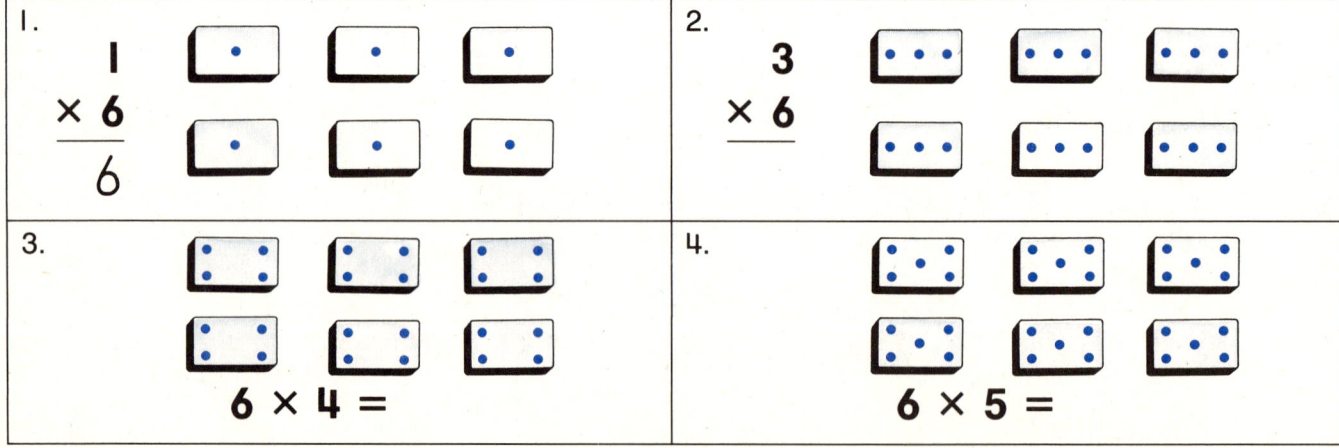

Practice

▸ Multiply.

1. $\begin{array}{r} 0 \\ \times\, 6 \\ \hline \end{array}$	2. $\begin{array}{r} 6 \\ \times\, 6 \\ \hline \end{array}$ ⚃⚃⚃⚃⚃⚃
3. $\begin{array}{r} 7 \\ \times\, 6 \\ \hline \end{array}$	4. $\begin{array}{r} 6 \\ \times\, 9 \\ \hline \end{array}$	5. $\begin{array}{r} 6 \\ \times\, 8 \\ \hline \end{array}$	6. $\begin{array}{r} 6 \\ \times\, 1 \\ \hline \end{array}$
7. $\begin{array}{r} 8 \\ \times\, 6 \\ \hline \end{array}$	8. $\begin{array}{r} 6 \\ \times\, 3 \\ \hline \end{array}$	9. $\begin{array}{r} 5 \\ \times\, 6 \\ \hline \end{array}$	10. $\begin{array}{r} 6 \\ \times\, 7 \\ \hline \end{array}$
11. $6 \times 6 =$	12. $9 \times 6 =$	13. $6 \times 3 =$	14. $7 \times 6 =$

Using Math

▸ There are 6 cans of fruit juice in a pack. Su Lei bought 6 packs. How many cans of juice did she buy in all?

She bought _____ cans in all.

Work here.

Multiplying by 7

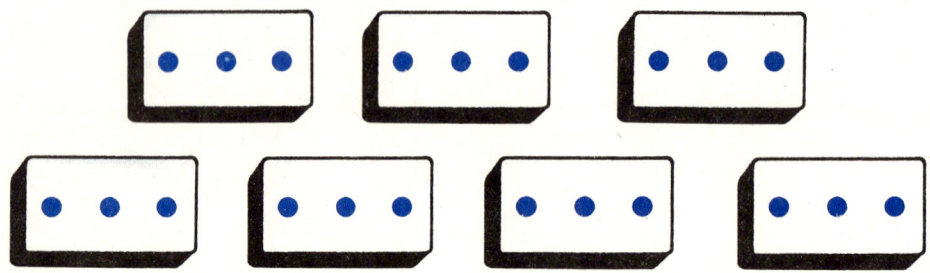

How many dots are there in all?

Step 1 Count the number in each group: 3.

Step 2 Count the groups: 7.

Step 3 Write: $7 \times 3 = 21$ or $\begin{array}{r} 3 \\ \times 7 \\ \hline 21 \end{array}$

Step 4 Say: There are 21 dots in all.

Guided Practice

▶ Multiply.

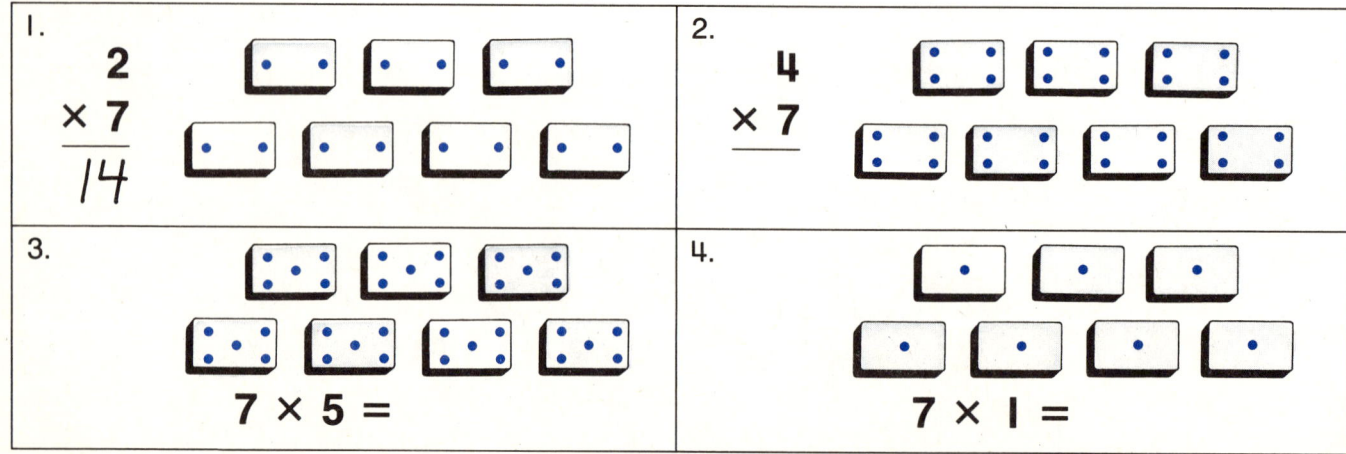

1. $\begin{array}{r} 2 \\ \times 7 \\ \hline 14 \end{array}$

2. $\begin{array}{r} 4 \\ \times 7 \\ \hline \end{array}$

3. $7 \times 5 =$

4. $7 \times 1 =$

Practice

▷ Multiply.

1. 6 × 7	2. 7 × 7

3. 7 × 8	4. 7 × 0	5. 9 × 7	6. 8 × 7
7. 7 × 6	8. 7 × 2	9. 0 × 7	10. 7 × 1
11. 7 × 7 =	12. 9 × 7 =	13. 7 × 5 =	14. 7 × 2 =

Using Math

▷ Sal has a flower garden. The garden has 7 rows with 8 plants in each row. How many plants are there in all?

There are _____ plants in all.

Work here.

101

3 Multiplying by 8

How many dots are there in all?

Step 1 — Count the number in each group: 4.

Step 2 — Count the groups: 8.

Step 3 — Write: 8 × 4 = 32   or $\begin{array}{r} 4 \\ \times\ 8 \\ \hline 32 \end{array}$

Step 4 — Say: There are 32 dots in all.

Guided Practice

▷ Multiply.

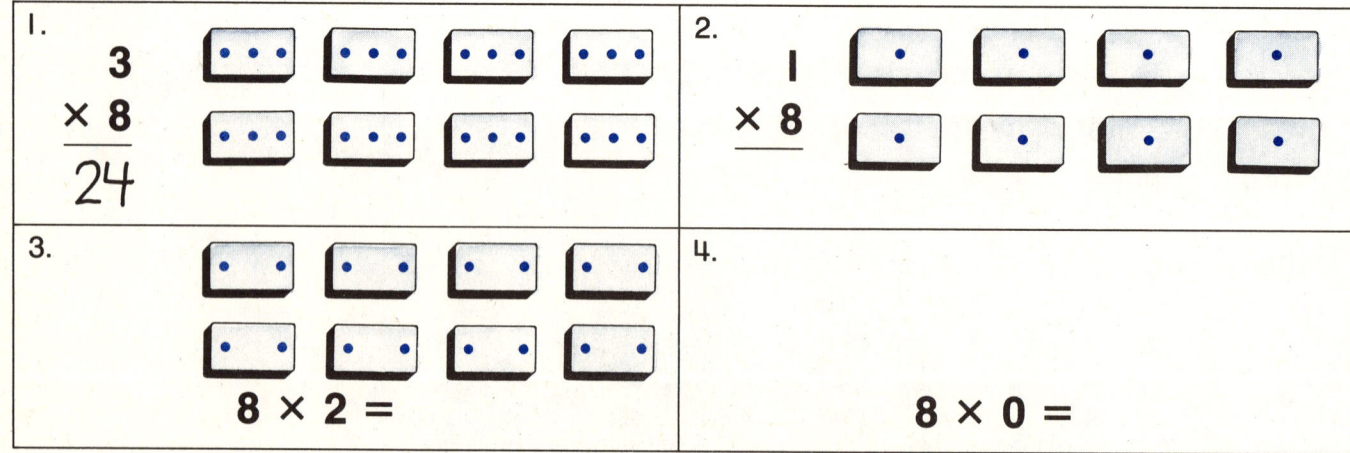

1. $\begin{array}{r} 3 \\ \times\ 8 \\ \hline 24 \end{array}$

2. $\begin{array}{r} 1 \\ \times\ 8 \\ \hline \end{array}$

3. 8 × 2 =

4. 8 × 0 =

102

Practice

▸ Multiply.

1. $\begin{array}{r}5\\ \times 8\\ \hline\end{array}$		2. $\begin{array}{r}6\\ \times 8\\ \hline\end{array}$	
3. $\begin{array}{r}8\\ \times 8\\ \hline\end{array}$	4. $\begin{array}{r}7\\ \times 8\\ \hline\end{array}$	5. $\begin{array}{r}9\\ \times 8\\ \hline\end{array}$	6. $\begin{array}{r}8\\ \times 0\\ \hline\end{array}$
7. $\begin{array}{r}4\\ \times 8\\ \hline\end{array}$	8. $\begin{array}{r}8\\ \times 6\\ \hline\end{array}$	9. $\begin{array}{r}8\\ \times 1\\ \hline\end{array}$	10. $\begin{array}{r}8\\ \times 5\\ \hline\end{array}$
11. $8 \times 7 =$	12. $2 \times 8 =$	13. $8 \times 9 =$	14. $8 \times 8 =$

Using Math

▸ Ron is reading a book. He has 8 chapters left. Each chapter has 8 pages. How many pages are left to read?

_____ pages are left to read.

Work here.

103

Multiplying by 9

How many dots are there in all?

Step 1 Count the number in each group: 5.

Step 2 Count the groups: 9.

Step 3 Write: 9 × 5 = 45   or $\begin{array}{r} 5 \\ \times\,9 \\ \hline 45 \end{array}$

Step 4 Say: There are 45 dots in all.

Guided Practice

▸ Multiply.

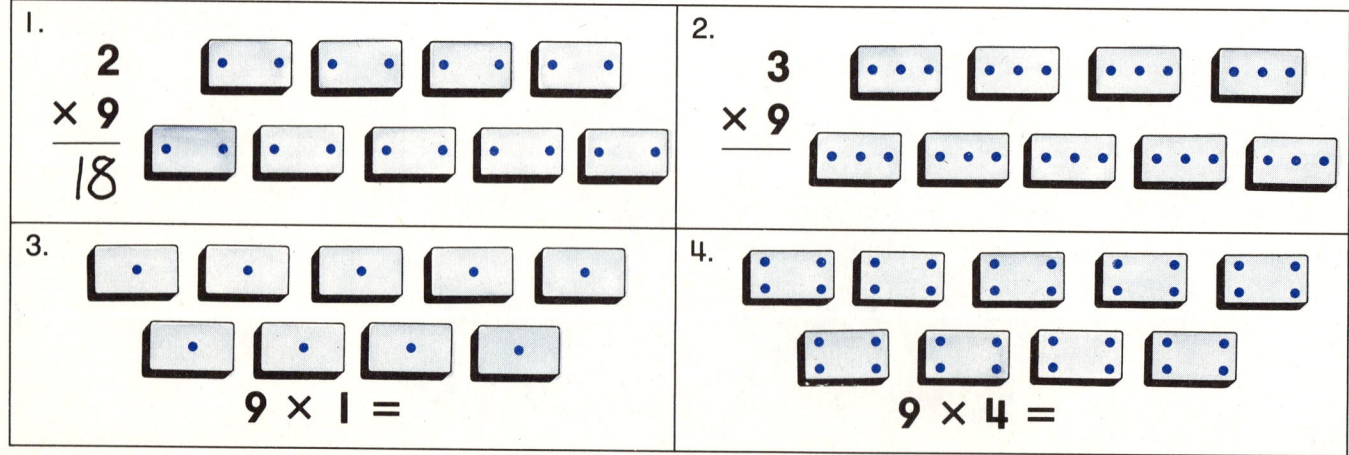

1. $\begin{array}{r} 2 \\ \times\,9 \\ \hline 18 \end{array}$

2. $\begin{array}{r} 3 \\ \times\,9 \\ \hline \end{array}$

3. 9 × 1 =

4. 9 × 4 =

Practice

▷ Multiply.

1. 7 × 9	2. 6 × 9		
3. 8 × 9	4. 9 × 5	5. 0 × 9	6. 9 × 4
7. 9 × 6	8. 9 × 2	9. 9 × 8	10. 9 × 7
11. 9 × 7 =	12. 9 × 8 =	13. 9 × 2 =	14. 9 × 9 =

Using Math

▷ John made 9 loaves of banana bread. He put 6 nuts on top of each loaf. How many nuts did he use in all?

He used _____ nuts in all.

Work here.

105

Multiplication Table 0-9

This multiplication table contains all the facts you have learned. Remember it can help you find the product of two factors.

×	0	1	2	3	4	5	6	7	8	9
0	0	0	0	0	0	0	0	0	0	0
1	0	1	2	3	4	5	6	7	8	9
2	0	2	4	6	8	10	12	14	16	18
3	0	3	6	9	12	15	18	21	24	27
4	0	4	8	12	16	20	24	28	32	36
5	0	5	10	15	20	25	30	35	40	45
6	0	6	12	18	24	30	36	42	48	54
7	0	7	14	21	28	35	42	49	56	63
8	0	8	16	24	32	40	48	56	64	72
9	0	9	18	27	36	45	54	63	72	81

This is how you use the table to find the product of 8 × 9.

Step 1 Find the first factor in the column under the ×.

Step 2 Move to the right until you are under the second factor.

Step 3 Read the product: 72.

Guided Practice

▶ Find each product using the multiplication table above.

1. 1 × 7 = 7	2. 2 × 0 =	3. 5 × 6 =
4. 3 × 7 =	5. 9 × 7 =	6. 4 × 8 =

Practice

▶ Multiply. You may use the multiplication table.

1. 8 × 7 =	2. 4 × 6 =	3. 3 × 8 =	4. 5 × 5 =
5. 0 × 2 =	6. 9 × 9 =	7. 7 × 7 =	8. 6 × 9 =
9. 6 × 7 =	10. 8 × 9 =	11. 5 × 4 =	12. 8 × 8 =
13. 3 × 9 =	14. 6 × 6 =	15. 2 × 3 =	16. 7 × 9 =
17. 9 × 1 =	18. 7 × 3 =	19. 0 × 6 =	20. 4 × 7 =
21. 3 × 4 =	22. 7 × 5 =	23. 8 × 6 =	24. 2 × 6 =

Problem Solving

▶ Write numbers to make the tables.

Burt paid 7¢ for a cupcake.
How much will 2, 3, 4, and 5 cupcakes cost?

Cupcake Prices

Cupcakes	1	2	3	4	5
Cost	7¢	___¢	___¢	___¢	___¢

Multiplication Facts 0–9

You know that the order of the factors does not change the product. So when you know one fact, you really know two!

3 × 2 = 6	2 × 3 = 6
4 × 3 = 12	3 × 4 = 12

Guided Practice

▶ Multiply.

1.
   4   2
× 2   × 4
――   ――
   8   8

2.
   1   3
× 3   × 1

3.
   3   5
× 5   × 3

4.
   5   4
× 4   × 5

5.
6 × 7 =
7 × 6 =

6.
6 × 2 =
2 × 6 =

108

Practice

▸ Multiply.

1. 9 × 8 8 × 9	2. 7 × 4 4 × 7	3. 6 × 5 5 × 6
4. 8 × 6 6 × 8	5. 7 × 9 9 × 7	6. 8 × 4 4 × 8
7. 9 × 3 3 × 9	8. 0 × 2 2 × 0	9. 9 × 6 6 × 9
10. 7 × 3 = 3 × 7 =	11. 5 × 8 = 8 × 5 =	12. 9 × 4 = 4 × 9 =

Using Math

▸ Use a fact pair to solve the problem.

The store clerk is filling up a case with cans of soup. She can put the cans in 6 rows with 4 cans in each row. Or she can make 4 rows with 6 cans in each row. Either way, how many cans of soup are there in a case?

There are _____ cans of soup in a case.

Work here.

Time to 5 Minutes

What time is it?

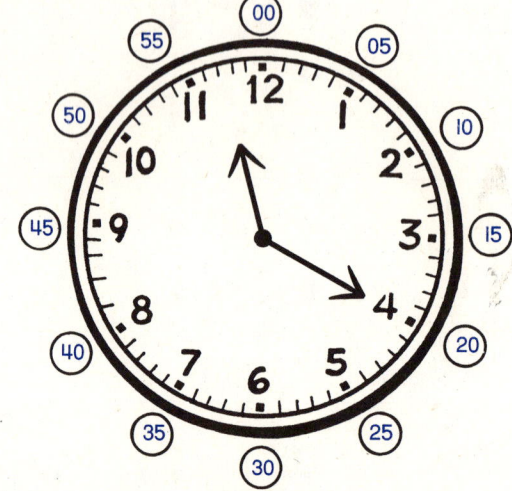

Step 1 Look at the hour hand. It is between 11 and 12. Remember that the smaller number tells the hour. The hour is 11.

Step 2 Look at the minute hand. It points to 4. This is 20 minutes. We write 20.

 The time is 11:20.

Guided Practice

Write each time.

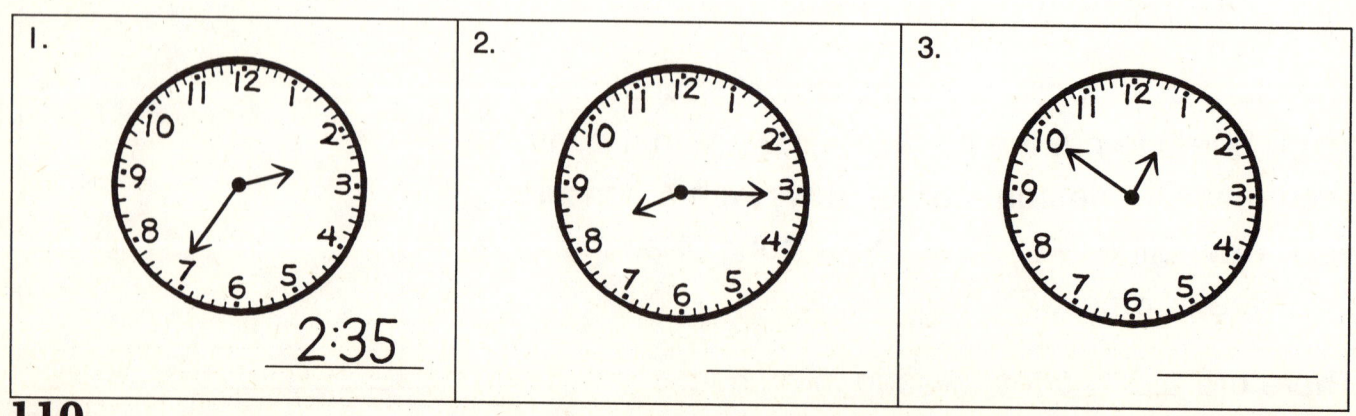

1. 2:35

2. _____

3. _____

Practice

▶ Write each time.

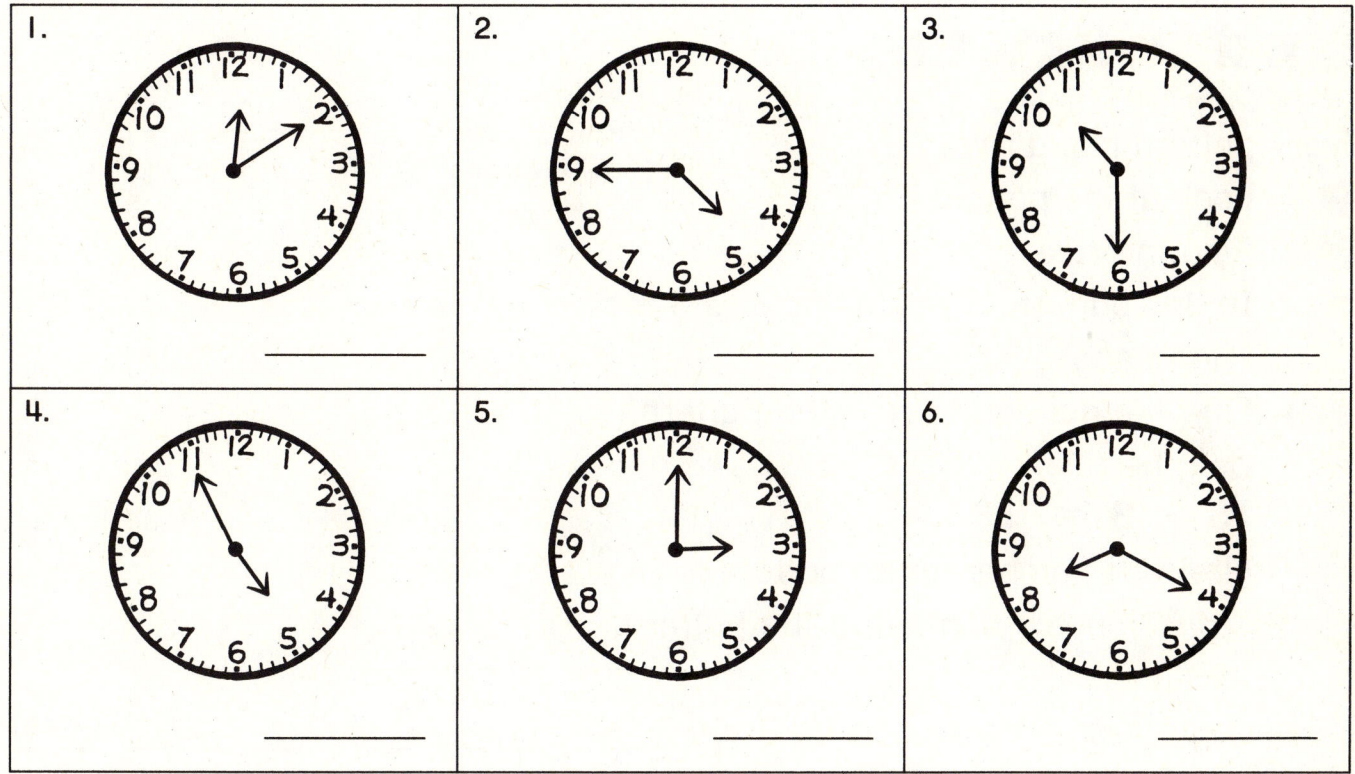

Using Math

▶ The store closes at 6:15.

What time does the clock show? _____

Has the store closed? Write **yes** or **no**. _____

Problem Solving

Find a Pattern

Every pattern has a rule.

Step 1 Look at the pattern.

| 3 | 6 | 9 | 12 | 15 | |

Step 2 Find the rule.

In this pattern, every number is 3 more.

The rule is __+3__.

Step 3 Find the next number in the pattern. Use the rule.

15 + 3 = __18__

The next number in the pattern is __18__.

Step 4 Write the next number in the pattern.

| 3 | 6 | 9 | 12 | 15 | 18 |

Guided Practice

▶ Find the rule in each pattern.
Write the next number.

1.
| 12 | 10 | 8 | 6 | 4 |

The rule is __-2__.

2.
| 5 | 10 | 15 | 20 | |

The rule is _____.

3.
| 2 | 4 | 6 | 8 | |

The rule is _____.

4.
| 10 | 9 | 8 | 7 | |

The rule is _____.

Practice

▶ Find the rule in each pattern.
Write the next number.

1. | 8 | 10 | 12 | 14 | |
The rule is _____.

2. | 6 | 12 | 18 | 24 | |
The rule is _____.

3. | 24 | 23 | 22 | 21 | |
The rule is _____.

4. | 15 | 20 | 25 | 30 | |
The rule is _____.

5. | 12 | 16 | 20 | 24 | |
The rule is _____.

6. | 16 | 14 | 12 | 10 | |
The rule is _____.

7. | 4 | 5 | 6 | 7 | |
The rule is _____.

8. | 6 | 9 | 12 | 15 | |
The rule is _____.

9. | 8 | 16 | 24 | 32 | |
The rule is _____.

10. | 9 | 18 | 27 | 36 | |
The rule is _____.

▶ Make your own patterns.
Write the rules.

11. | | | | | |
The rule is _____.

12. | | | | | |
The rule is _____.

CHAPTER 5 Review

Multiply.

pages 98–99

1. 5 × 6
2. 3 × 6
3. 6 × 6
4. 7 × 6
5. 2 × 6
6. 4 × 6
7. 1 × 6
8. 9 × 6

pages 100–101

9. 9 × 7
10. 6 × 7
11. 2 × 7
12. 4 × 7
13. 3 × 7
14. 8 × 7
15. 0 × 7
16. 5 × 7

pages 102–103

17. 6 × 8
18. 2 × 8
19. 9 × 8
20. 5 × 8
21. 4 × 8
22. 1 × 8
23. 3 × 8
24. 8 × 8

CHAPTER 5 Review

▶ Multiply.

pages 104–105

| 25. 6 × 9 | 26. 0 × 9 | 27. 2 × 9 | 28. 9 × 9 |
| 29. 3 × 9 | 30. 5 × 9 | 31. 4 × 9 | 32. 7 × 9 |

pages 108–109

| 33. 5 × 2   2 × 5 | 34. 4 × 3   3 × 4 | 35. 6 × 5   5 × 6 |
| 36. 2 × 0   0 × 2 | 37. 8 × 7   7 × 8 | 38. 9 × 4   4 × 9 |

▶ Write each time.
pages 110–111

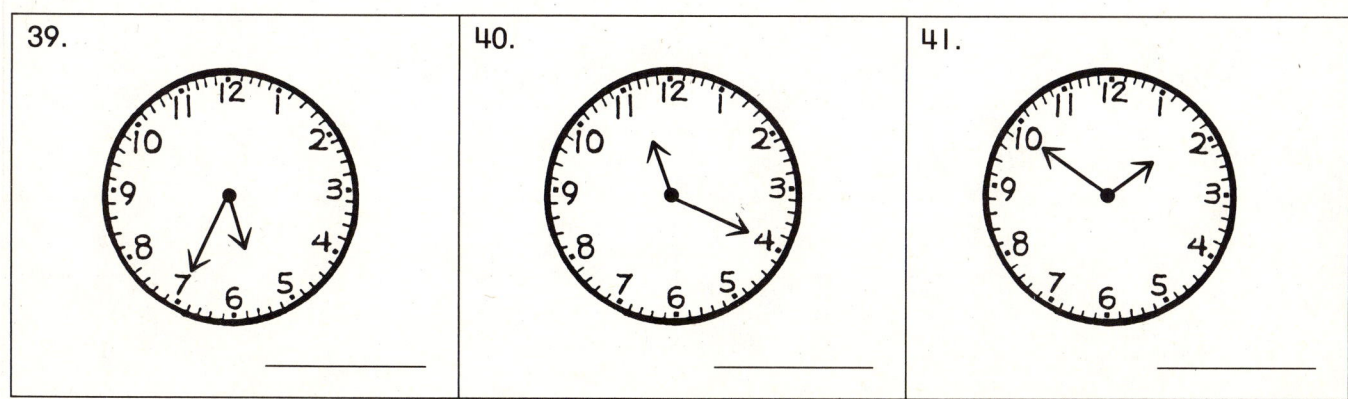

115

CHAPTER 5 Review

▶ Find the rule in each pattern.
Write the next number. pages 112–113

42. | 1 | 3 | 5 | 7 | |

The rule is _____.

43. | 7 | 9 | 11 | 13 | |

The rule is _____.

44. | 24 | 20 | 16 | 12 | |

The rule is _____.

45. | 15 | 14 | 13 | 12 | |

The rule is _____.

46. | 30 | 25 | 20 | 15 | |

The rule is _____.

47. | 10 | 20 | 30 | 40 | |

The rule is _____.

48. | 20 | 23 | 26 | 29 | |

The rule is _____.

49. | 4 | 8 | 12 | 16 | |

The rule is _____.

50. | 60 | 50 | 40 | 30 | |

The rule is _____.

51. | 22 | 24 | 26 | 28 | |

The rule is _____.

▶ Make your own patterns.
Write the rules.

52. | | | | | |

The rule is _____.

53. | | | | | |

The rule is _____.

116

CHAPTER 5 Test

▶ Multiply.

1. 8 × 6	2. 7 × 6	3. 9 × 6	4. 4 × 6
5. 5 × 7	6. 7 × 7	7. 4 × 7	8. 3 × 7
9. 7 × 8	10. 5 × 8	11. 8 × 8	12. 4 × 8
13. 9 × 9	14. 7 × 9	15. 8 × 9	16. 6 × 9

▶ Write each time.

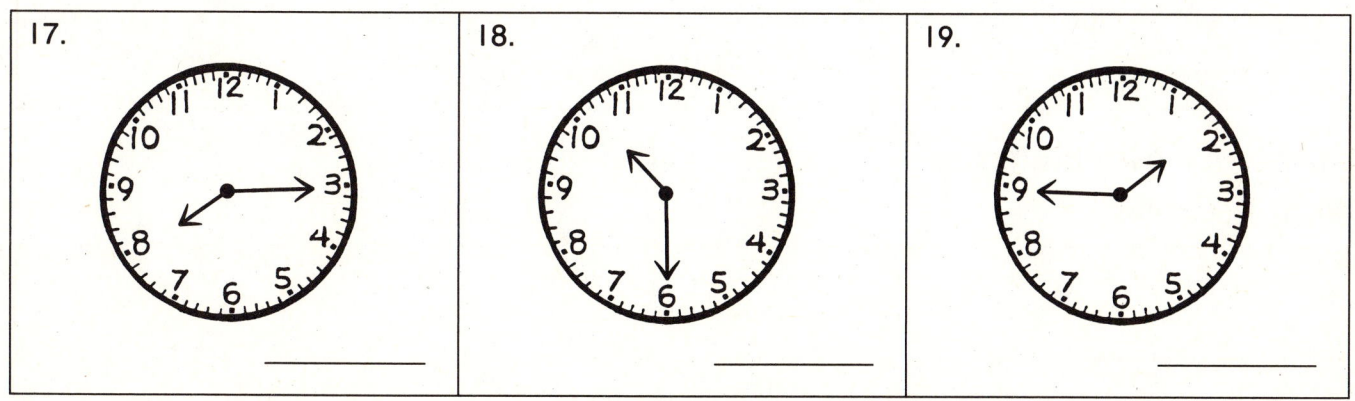

17.   18.   19.

117

Test

▶ Find the rule in each pattern.
Write the next number.

20. | 4 | 6 | 8 | 10 | |

The rule is _____.

21. | 15 | 12 | 9 | 6 | |

The rule is _____.

22. | 7 | 6 | 5 | 4 | |

The rule is _____.

23. | 3 | 6 | 9 | 12 | |

The rule is _____.

24. | 22 | 26 | 30 | 34 | |

The rule is _____.

25. | 13 | 14 | 15 | 16 | |

The rule is _____.

26. | 7 | 9 | 11 | 13 | |

The rule is _____.

27. | 24 | 20 | 16 | 12 | |

The rule is _____.

28. | 50 | 60 | 70 | 80 | |

The rule is _____.

29. | 9 | 18 | 27 | 36 | |

The rule is _____.

▶ Make your own patterns.
Write the rules.

30. | | | | | |

The rule is _____.

31. | | | | | |

The rule is _____.

CHAPTER 6
Division Facts Through 6

Four friends earned 28 dollars helping the neighbors after school. They want to share the money equally. How much should each friend get?

 Solve

▷ Write a problem about something you can share.

Dividing by 2

You can subtract to find how many groups of 2 are in 6.

$6 - 2 = 4$ $4 - 2 = 2$ $2 - 2 = 0$

There are 3 groups of 2 in 6.

You can also **divide** to find how many **twos** are in 6.

Step 1 Count:

Step 2 Divide:

6 divided by 2 equals 3.

Step 3 Write: $2\overline{)6}^{\,3}$ or $6 \div 2 = 3$

Step 4 Say: There are 3 **twos** in 6.

Guided Practice

▶ Divide.

1. $2\overline{)4}^{\,2}$ 	2. $2\overline{)8}$  
3. $4 \div 2 =$	4. $8 \div 2 =$

Practice

▶ Divide.

1. $2\overline{)10}$	2. $2\overline{)12}$
3. $2\overline{)4}$	4. $2\overline{)14}$	5. $2\overline{)16}$
6. $2\overline{)6}$	7. $2\overline{)18}$	8. $2\overline{)2}$
9. $8 \div 2 =$	10. $6 \div 2 =$	11. $14 \div 2 =$

Problem Solving

▶ Find the rule in the pattern.
Write the next number.

| 6 | 9 | 12 | 15 | |

The rule is _____.

2
Dividing by 3

You can subtract to find how many groups of 3 are in 9.

9 − 3 = 6   6 − 3 = 3   3 − 3 = 0

There are 3 groups of 3 in 9.

You can also **divide** to find how many **threes** are in 9.

Step 1 ▶ Count:

Step 2 ▶ Divide:

9 divided by 3 equals 3.

Step 3 ▶ Write: $3\overline{)9}$ with quotient 3   or   9 ÷ 3 = 3

Step 4 ▶ Say: There are 3 **threes** in 9.

Guided Practice

▶ Divide.

1. $3\overline{)12}$ with quotient 4

2. $3\overline{)6}$

3. 12 ÷ 3 =

4. 6 ÷ 3 =

Practice

Divide.

1. 3)15		2. 3)18
3. 3)3	4. 3)18	5. 3)24
6. 3)6	7. 3)27	8. 3)9
9. 12 ÷ 3 =	10. 15 ÷ 3 =	11. 24 ÷ 3 =

Using Math

Pam has 27 beanbags.
She will give each player 3 beanbags.
How many players can there be at the same time?

There can be _____ players.

Work here.

Dividing by 4

How many **fours** are in 20?

You can use a multiplication fact to answer this division question.

Multiplying Fours				
1 × 4 = 4	2 × 4 = 8	3 × 4 = 12	4 × 4 = 16	**5 × 4 = 20**
6 × 4 = 24	7 × 4 = 28	8 × 4 = 32	9 × 4 = 36	

There are 5 **fours** in 20.

Multiplication fact: 5 × 4 = 20   Division fact: 20 ÷ 4 = 5   or $4\overline{)20}$ = 5

Guided Practice

▶ Divide. Use the multiplication fact to help you.

1. 2 × 4 = __8__

    $4\overline{)8} = 2$

2. 3 × 4 = ____

    $4\overline{)12}$

3. 2 × 4 = ____

    8 ÷ 4 = ____

4. 3 × 4 = ____

    12 ÷ 4 = ____

Practice

▸ Divide.

1. 4)4	2. 4)16	3. 4)24
4. 4)20	5. 4)32	6. 4)28
7. 4)36	8. 4)12	9. 4)8
10. 32 ÷ 4 =	11. 24 ÷ 4 =	12. 4 ÷ 4 =

Using Math

▸ Michael has 32 tickets. Each ride costs 4 tickets. How many rides can Michael go on?

Michael can go on _____ rides.

Work here.

4

Dividing by 5

How many **fives** are in 15?

You can use a multiplication fact to answer this division question.

Multiplying Fives			
1 × 5 = 5	2 × 5 = 10	3 × 5 = 15	4 × 5 = 20	5 × 5 = 25
6 × 5 = 30	7 × 5 = 35	8 × 5 = 40	9 × 5 = 45	

There are 3 **fives** in 15.

Multiplication fact: 3 × 5 = 15   Division fact: 15 ÷ 5 = 3   or   5)15̄ = 3

Guided Practice

▸ Divide. Use the multiplication fact to help you.

1. 2 × 5 = __10__

   5)10̄ = 2

2. 1 × 5 = ____

   5)5̄

3. 2 × 5 = ____

   10 ÷ 5 = ____

4. 1 × 5 = ____

   5 ÷ 5 = ____

Practice

Divide.

1. $5\overline{)5}$	2. $5\overline{)20}$	3. $5\overline{)25}$
4. $5\overline{)35}$	5. $5\overline{)45}$	6. $5\overline{)30}$
7. $5\overline{)40}$	8. $5\overline{)10}$	9. $5\overline{)15}$
10. $35 \div 5 =$	11. $30 \div 5 =$	12. $20 \div 5 =$

Using Math

Maria bought 5 tickets for the carnival games. She paid 40¢ in all. How much did each ticket cost?

Each ticket cost _____ ¢.

Work here.

 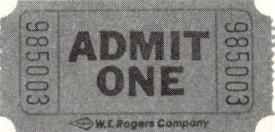 

Dividing by 6

How many **sixes** are in 18?

Multiplying Sixes				
1 × 6 = 6	2 × 6 = 12	3 × 6 = 18	4 × 6 = 24	5 × 6 = 30
6 × 6 = 36	7 × 6 = 42		8 × 6 = 48	9 × 6 = 54

There are 3 **sixes** in 18.

Multiplication fact: 3 × 6 = 18   Division fact: 18 ÷ 6 = 3   or $6\overline{)18}$ = 3

Guided Practice

▶ Divide. Use the multiplication fact to help you.

1. 2 × 6 = __12__

   $6\overline{)12}$ = 2

2. 1 × 6 = ____

   $6\overline{)6}$

3. 2 × 6 = ____

   12 ÷ 6 = ____

4. 1 × 6 = ____

   6 ÷ 6 = ____

Practice

Divide.

1. $6\overline{)54}$	2. $6\overline{)48}$	3. $6\overline{)12}$
4. $6\overline{)18}$	5. $6\overline{)36}$	6. $6\overline{)6}$
7. $6\overline{)42}$	8. $6\overline{)24}$	9. $6\overline{)30}$
10. $54 \div 6 =$	11. $42 \div 6 =$	12. $36 \div 6 =$

Using Math

There are 36 students on floats in the school parade. 6 students are on each float. How many floats are there?

There are _____ floats.

Work here.

Multiplication and Division Facts

You know that multiplication facts can be used to find division facts. Study the examples.

Twos	1 × 2 = 2 2 ÷ 2 = 1	3 × 2 = 6 6 ÷ 2 = 3	5 × 2 = 10 10 ÷ 2 = 5	7 × 2 = 14 14 ÷ 2 = 7
Threes	1 × 3 = 3 3 ÷ 3 = 1	2 × 3 = 6 6 ÷ 3 = 2	4 × 3 = 12 12 ÷ 3 = 4	6 × 3 = 18 18 ÷ 3 = 6
Fours	1 × 4 = 4 4 ÷ 4 = 1	4 × 4 = 16 16 ÷ 4 = 4	7 × 4 = 28 28 ÷ 4 = 7	9 × 4 = 36 36 ÷ 4 = 9
Fives	1 × 5 = 5 5 ÷ 5 = 1	3 × 5 = 15 15 ÷ 5 = 3	6 × 5 = 30 30 ÷ 5 = 6	9 × 5 = 45 45 ÷ 5 = 9
Sixes	1 × 6 = 6 6 ÷ 6 = 1	2 × 6 = 12 12 ÷ 6 = 2	6 × 6 = 36 36 ÷ 6 = 6	8 × 6 = 48 48 ÷ 6 = 8

Guided Practice

▶ Multiply. Then divide.

1. 2 × 2 = __4__
   4 ÷ 2 = __2__

2. 3 × 3 = ____
   9 ÷ 3 = ____

3. 5 × 4 = ____
   20 ÷ 4 = ____

4. 7 × 5 = ____
   35 ÷ 5 = ____

5. 4 × 6 = ____
   24 ÷ 6 = ____

6. 4 × 3 = ____
   12 ÷ 3 = ____

Practice

Multiply. Then divide.

1. $4 \times 2 = \underline{}$ $8 \div 2 = \underline{}$	2. $5 \times 3 = \underline{}$ $15 \div 3 = \underline{}$	3. $2 \times 4 = \underline{}$ $8 \div 4 = \underline{}$
4. $7 \times 3 = \underline{}$ $21 \div 3 = \underline{}$	5. $8 \times 4 = \underline{}$ $32 \div 4 = \underline{}$	6. $2 \times 5 = \underline{}$ $10 \div 5 = \underline{}$
7. $8 \times 5 = \underline{}$ $40 \div 5 = \underline{}$	8. $8 \times 3 = \underline{}$ $24 \div 3 = \underline{}$	9. $3 \times 6 = \underline{}$ $18 \div 6 = \underline{}$
10. $7 \times 6 = \underline{}$ $42 \div 6 = \underline{}$	11. $9 \times 4 = \underline{}$ $36 \div 4 = \underline{}$	12. $9 \times 6 = \underline{}$ $54 \div 6 = \underline{}$

Using Math

Carlos bought 5 buttons for 35¢. How much did he pay for each button?

Carlos paid ____¢ for each button.

Work here.

The Digital Clock

A **digital clock** is another kind of clock.
The numbers on a digital clock look like this.

0 1 2 3 4 5 6 7 8 9 10 11 12

It is easy to tell time on a digital clock once you can read the numbers. Can you tell the time on this digital clock? The time is 9:10.

Guided Practice

▷ Match.

Practice

▸ Match.

1. 11:30	2. 4:00	3. 12:40
4. 3:30	5. 1:55	6. 5:40
7. 9:05	8. 2:35	9. 6:00

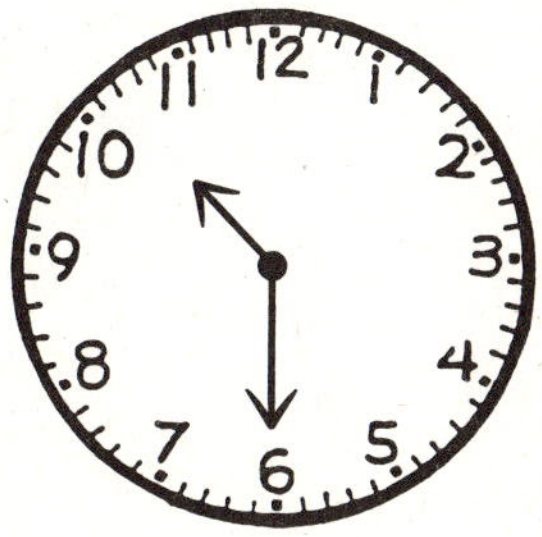

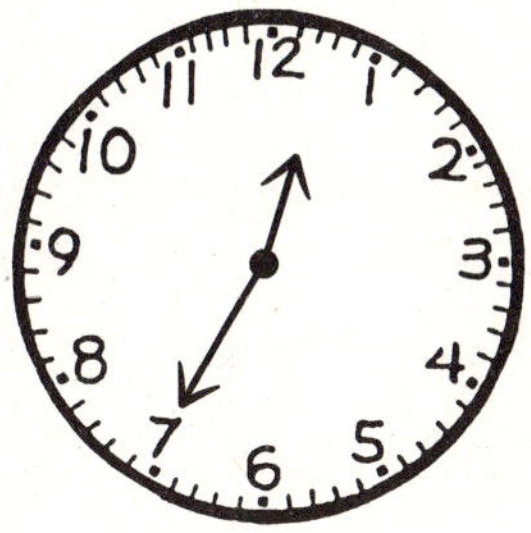

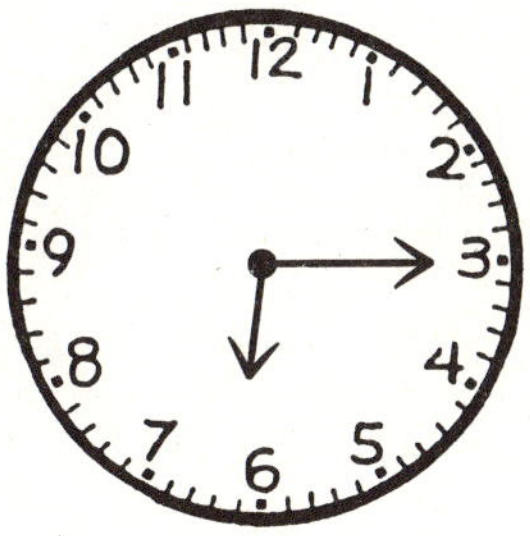

Using Math

▸ Matt sets his watch by his digital clock. Draw the hands on Matt's watch so they tell the same time as the digital clock.

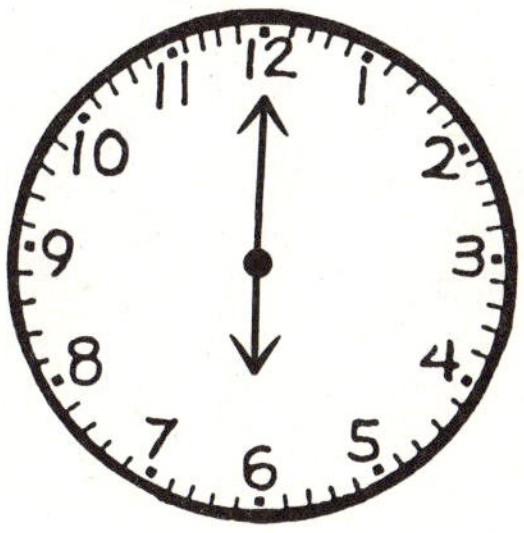

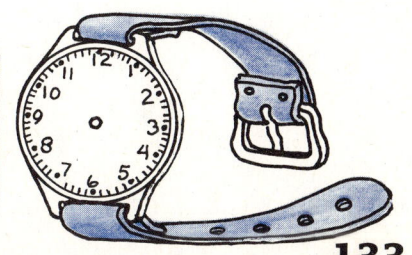

133

Problem Solving

Find a Pattern

Remember that all patterns have a rule.

Step 1 Look at the pattern.
Step 2 Find the rule.
In this pattern,
every number is divided by 3.
The rule is ÷ 3 .

Step 3 Find the next number in the pattern.
Use the rule.
12 ÷ 3 = 4
The next number in the pattern is 4 .

Step 4 Write the number
in the pattern.

3	1
6	2
9	3
12	

3	1
6	2
9	3
12	4

Guided Practice

Find the rule in each pattern.
Write the next number.

1. | 2 | 10 |
    | 3 | 15 |
    | 4 | 20 |
    The rule is ×5 .

2. | 1 | 2 |
    | 2 | 4 |
    | 3 | |
    The rule is _____ .

3. | 12 | 3 |
    | 16 | 4 |
    | 20 | |
    The rule is _____ .

4. | 6 | 3 |
    | 8 | 4 |
    | 10 | |
    The rule is _____ .

Practice

▶ Find the rule in each pattern.
Write the next number.

1. | 2 | 8 |
    | 3 | 12 |
    | 4 | |
    The rule is ____.

2. | 3 | 3 |
    | 4 | 4 |
    | 5 | |
    The rule is ____.

3. | 6 | 2 |
    | 9 | 3 |
    | 12 | |
    The rule is ____.

4. | 8 | 4 |
    | 10 | 5 |
    | 12 | |
    The rule is ____.

5. | 10 | 2 |
    | 15 | 3 |
    | 20 | |
    The rule is ____.

6. | 16 | 4 |
    | 12 | 3 |
    | 8 | |
    The rule is ____.

7. | 3 | 6 |
    | 4 | 8 |
    | 5 | |
    The rule is ____.

8. | 1 | 3 |
    | 2 | 6 |
    | 3 | |
    The rule is ____.

9. | 2 | 12 |
    | 3 | 18 |
    | 4 | |
    The rule is ____.

10. | 6 | 1 |
    | 12 | 2 |
    | 18 | |
    The rule is ____.

▶ Find the rule in each pattern. Write the next number pair.

11. | 1 | 2 |
    | 2 | 4 |
    | 3 | 6 |
    The rule is ____.

12. | 1 | 5 |
    | 2 | 10 |
    | 3 | 15 |
    The rule is ____.

135

CHAPTER 6 Review

▶ Divide.

pages 120–121 1. 2)16	2. 2)8	3. 2)12	4. 2)18
5. 2)14	6. 2)10	7. 2)2	8. 2)4
pages 122–123 9. 3)3	10. 3)24	11. 3)9	12. 3)15
13. 3)18	14. 3)12	15. 3)6	16. 3)27
pages 124–125 17. 4)32	18. 4)24	19. 4)16	20. 4)36
21. 4)4	22. 4)12	23. 4)28	24. 4)8

CHAPTER 6 Review

▸ Divide.

pages 126–127

25. 5)20
26. 5)15
27. 5)40
28. 5)25

29. 5)45
30. 5)30
31. 5)10
32. 5)35

pages 128–129

33. 6)12
34. 6)48
35. 6)30
36. 6)42

37. 6)24
38. 6)36
39. 6)18
40. 6)54

▸ Match. pages 132–133

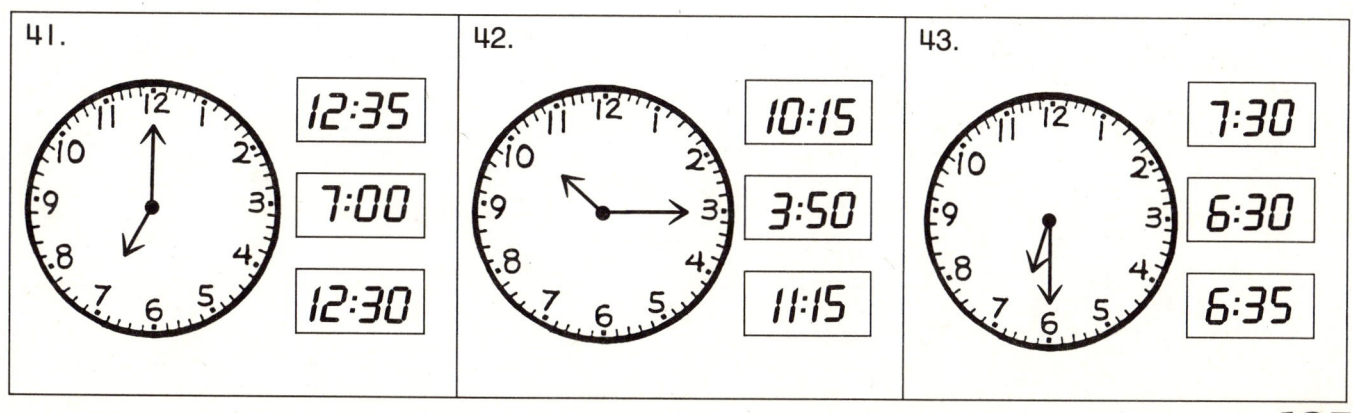

137

CHAPTER 6 Review

▶ Find the rule in each pattern. Write the next number. pages 134–135

44.
1	3
2	6
3	

The rule is _____.

45.
2	8
4	16
6	

The rule is _____.

46.
6	3
8	4
10	

The rule is _____.

47.
3	9
4	12
5	

The rule is _____.

48.
2	6
3	9
4	

The rule is _____.

49.
5	1
10	2
15	

The rule is _____.

50.
1	1
2	2
3	

The rule is _____.

51.
4	12
5	15
6	

The rule is _____.

52.
10	2
15	3
20	

The rule is _____.

53.
1	2
4	8
8	

The rule is _____.

▶ Find the rule in each pattern. Write the next number pair.

54.
1	3
2	6
3	9

The rule is _____.

55.
1	10
2	20
3	30

The rule is _____.

138

CHAPTER 6 Test

▸ Divide.

1. $2\overline{)14}$	2. $2\overline{)8}$	3. $3\overline{)6}$	4. $3\overline{)18}$
5. $4\overline{)20}$	6. $4\overline{)12}$	7. $4\overline{)36}$	8. $4\overline{)28}$
9. $5\overline{)45}$	10. $5\overline{)10}$	11. $5\overline{)30}$	12. $5\overline{)20}$
13. $6\overline{)18}$	14. $6\overline{)42}$	15. $6\overline{)24}$	16. $6\overline{)48}$

▸ Match.

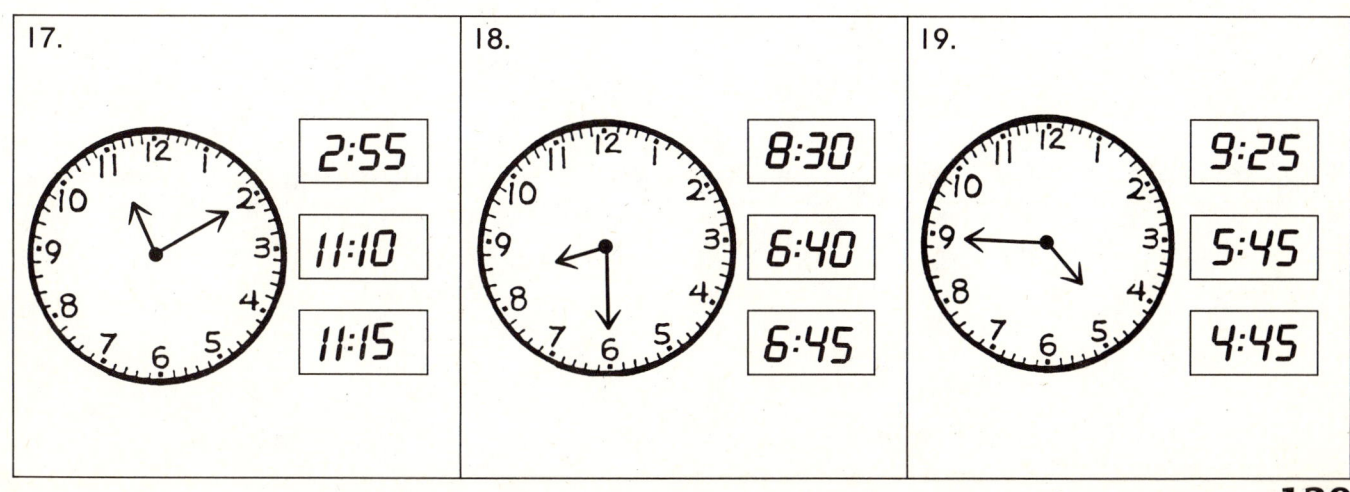

139

CHAPTER  Test

▶ Find the rule in each pattern. Write the next number.

20.
1	3
2	6
3	

The rule is _____.

21.
4	2
6	3
8	

The rule is _____.

22.
4	16
5	20
6	

The rule is _____.

23.
2	12
3	18
4	

The rule is _____.

24.
8	4
10	5
12	

The rule is _____.

25.
1	8
2	16
3	

The rule is _____.

26.
6	3
8	4
10	

The rule is _____.

27.
3	9
4	12
5	

The rule is _____.

28.
5	1
10	2
15	

The rule is _____.

29.
2	20
3	30
4	

The rule is _____.

▶ Find the rule in each pattern. Write the next two number pairs.

30.
1	1
2	2
3	3

The rule is _____.

31.
1	4
2	8
3	12

The rule is _____.

140

CHAPTER  Cumulative Review

▸ Multiply.

pages 76–79			
1. 5 × 2	2. 9 × 2	3. 4 × 3	4. 7 × 3

pages 80–81			
5. 6 × 4	6. 8 × 4	7. 2 × 4	8. 7 × 4

pages 82–83			
9. 7 × 5	10. 9 × 5	11. 6 × 5	12. 4 × 5

pages 84–85			
13. 2 × 0	14. 8 × 1	15. 3 × 1	16. 8 × 0

▸ Draw the hands on each clock to show the time. pages 88–89

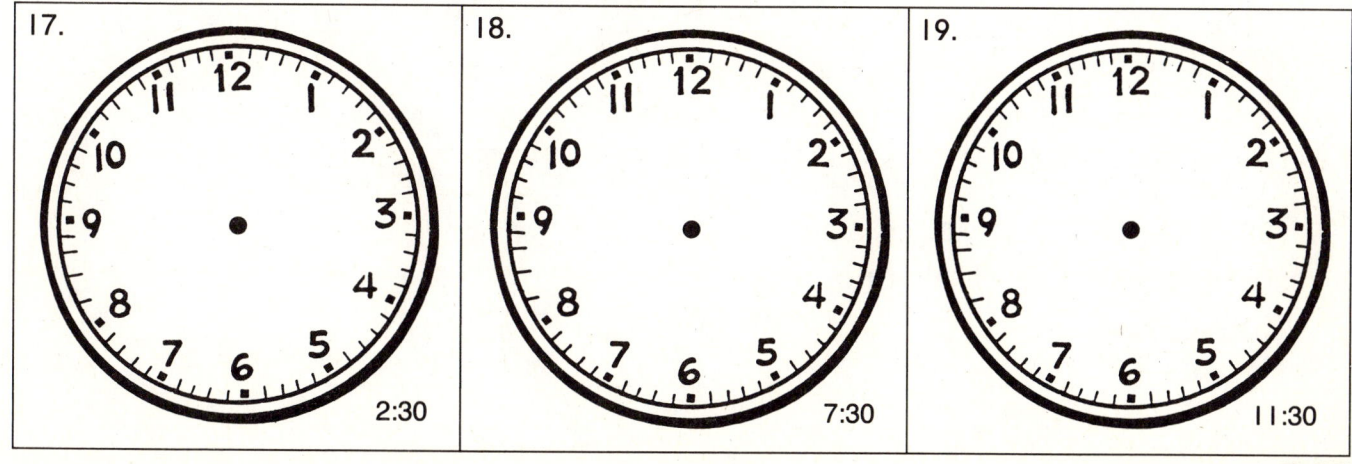

17. 2:30   18. 7:30   19. 11:30

141

CHAPTER  Cumulative Review

Write numbers to make the tables. pages 90–91

20. Kyle bought a sports magazine for 1¢.
How much will 2, 3, and 4 magazines cost?

Magazine Prices

Magazines	1	2	3	4
Cost	1¢	___¢	___¢	___¢

21. Maria paid 3¢ for a book.
How much will 2, 3, and 4 books cost?

Book Prices

Books	1	2	3	4
Cost	3¢	___¢	___¢	___¢

22. Kate bought a newspaper for 5¢.
How much will 2, 3, and 4 newspapers cost?

Newspaper Prices

Newspapers	1	2	3	4
Cost	5¢	___¢	___¢	___¢

23. Sheila paid 6¢ for a music magazine.
How much will 2, 3, and 4 magazines cost?

Music Magazine Prices

Magazines	1	2	3	4
Cost	6¢	___¢	___¢	___¢

24. Paul paid 8¢ for a comic book.
How much will 2, 3, 4, and 5 books cost?

Comic Book Prices

Comic Books	1	2	3	4	5
Cost	8¢	___¢	___¢	___¢	___¢

CHAPTER 5 Cumulative Review

▸ Multiply.

pages 98–99			
1. 6 ×6	2. 8 ×6	3. 5 ×6	4. 3 ×6

pages 100–101			
5. 4 ×7	6. 9 ×7	7. 6 ×7	8. 8 ×7

pages 102–103			
9. 3 ×8	10. 5 ×8	11. 6 ×8	12. 8 ×0

pages 104–105			
13. 4 ×9	14. 8 ×9	15. 1 ×9	16. 6 ×9

▸ Write each time.   pages 110–111

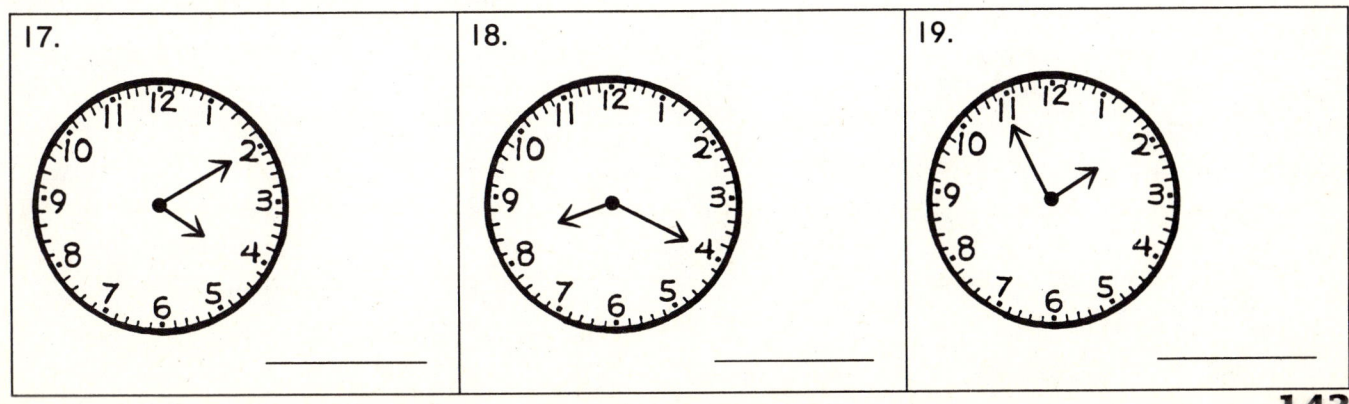

17.

18.

19.

143

CHAPTER 5 Cumulative Review

▸ Find the rule in each pattern.
Write the next number. pages 112–113

20. | 5 | 6 | 7 | 8 | |

The rule is _____.

21. | 24 | 23 | 22 | 21 | |

The rule is _____.

22. | 12 | 14 | 16 | 18 | |

The rule is _____.

23. | 12 | 18 | 24 | 30 | |

The rule is _____.

24. | 21 | 19 | 17 | 15 | |

The rule is _____.

25. | 15 | 20 | 25 | 30 | |

The rule is _____.

26. | 30 | 40 | 50 | 60 | |

The rule is _____.

27. | 35 | 30 | 25 | 20 | |

The rule is _____.

28. | 0 | 6 | 12 | 18 | |

The rule is _____.

29. | 8 | 16 | 24 | 32 | |

The rule is _____.

▸ Make your own patterns.
Write the rules.

30.

The rule is _____.

31.

The rule is _____.

144

CHAPTER 6 Cumulative Review

▶ Divide.

pages 120–123			
1. $2\overline{)14}$	2. $2\overline{)18}$	3. $3\overline{)15}$	4. $3\overline{)27}$

pages 124–125			
5. $4\overline{)16}$	6. $4\overline{)8}$	7. $4\overline{)24}$	8. $4\overline{)32}$

pages 126–127			
9. $5\overline{)30}$	10. $5\overline{)15}$	11. $5\overline{)25}$	12. $5\overline{)35}$

pages 128–129			
13. $6\overline{)24}$	14. $6\overline{)48}$	15. $6\overline{)12}$	16. $6\overline{)36}$

▶ Match. pages 132–133

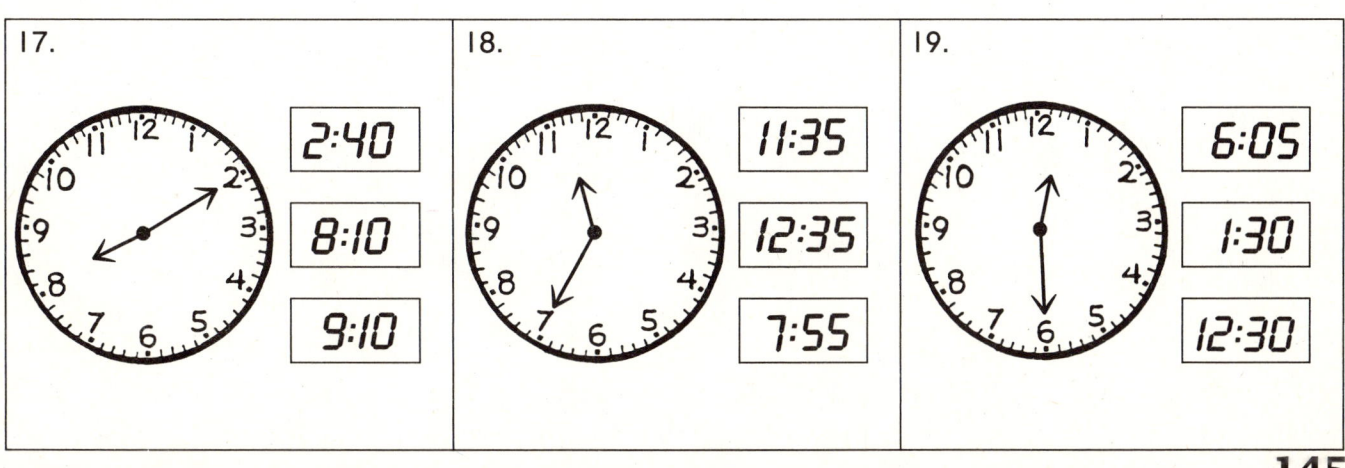

145

CHAPTER 6 Cumulative Review

▶ Find the rule in each pattern. Write the next number. pages 134–135

20.
1	2
2	4
3	

The rule is ____.

21.
4	12
5	15
6	

The rule is ____.

22.
5	1
10	2
15	

The rule is ____.

23.
1	7
2	14
3	

The rule is ____.

24.
8	1
16	2
24	

The rule is ____.

25.
2	8
3	12
4	

The rule is ____.

26.
40	4
30	3
20	

The rule is ____.

27.
1	9
2	18
3	

The rule is ____.

28.
9	9
10	10
11	

The rule is ____.

29.
5	25
6	30
7	

The rule is ____.

▶ Find the rule in each pattern. Write the next number pair.

30.
2	4
4	8
6	12

The rule is ____.

31.
1	5
2	10
3	15

The rule is ____.

CHAPTER 1 Extra Practice

Add.

pages 2–5
1. 3 + 6
2. 4 + 3
3. 3 + 8
4. 7 + 7

pages 6–7
5. 9 + 9
6. 8 + 7
7. 8 + 9
8. 7 + 9

Subtract.

pages 8–9
9. 5 − 2
10. 8 − 4
11. 10 − 7
12. 9 − 3

pages 10–11
13. 13 − 5
14. 11 − 8
15. 14 − 6
16. 12 − 7

pages 12–13
17. 17 − 8
18. 15 − 9
19. 18 − 9
20. 16 − 7

Write the day that completes each sentence. pages 14–15

21. The day before Sunday is _____.
    Saturday   Monday

22. The day after Sunday is _____.
    Saturday   Monday

CHAPTER 1 Extra Practice

▶ Make a drawing to solve. pages 16–17

23. Eve bought 4 cartons of milk. Calvin bought 3 cartons of milk. How many cartons in all did they buy?

☐ + ☐

_____ cartons in all

24. Carla used 8 oranges to make orange juice. She used 5 oranges to make fruit salad. How many oranges in all did she use?

☐ + ☐

_____ oranges in all

25. Andy put 6 boxes of cereal on a shelf. He put 6 boxes of cookies on a shelf. How many boxes in all are there?

_____ boxes in all

26. Lindsey put 7 books on a shelf. Claire put 2 books on a shelf. How many books in all are there?

_____ books in all

148

CHAPTER 2 Extra Practice

▷ Write each number. pages 24–25

1. 5 tens 0 ones = _____
2. 2 tens 5 ones = _____

pages 26–27

3. 7 hundreds 0 tens 3 ones = _____
4. 9 hundreds 7 tens 3 ones = _____

pages 28–29

5. 800 + 20 + 6 = _____
6. 100 + 90 = _____

pages 30–31

7. 4 thousands 6 hundreds 8 tens 2 ones = _____

8. 9 thousands 7 hundreds 0 tens 3 ones = _____

pages 32–33

9. 4,000 + 500 + 60 + 7 = _____
10. 7,000 + 400 + 9 = _____

▷ Compare. Ring > or <. pages 34–35

11. 33 (>/<) 32
12. 127 (</>) 137
13. 856 (</>) 845

▷ Use the June calendar to answer each question. pages 36–37

June

Sunday	Monday	Tuesday	Wednesday	Thursday	Friday	Saturday
		1	2	3	4	5
6	7	8	9	10	11	12
13	14	15	16	17	18	19
20	21	22	23	24	25	26
27	28	29	30			

14. On what day does June begin? _____

15. What is the date of the first Sunday in June? _____

CHAPTER 2 Extra Practice

Make a drawing to solve. pages 38–39

16. Gail rode the bus for 8 blocks from her house.
    She got off the bus and walked 5 more blocks from
    the bus stop to the school.
    How many blocks was she from her house?

    Answer _____ blocks.

17. Carol and Ben rode their bikes 7 blocks from home to the park.
    Ben rode back to his house.
    How many blocks in all did Ben ride?

    Answer _____ blocks.

18. David and Carlos live 9 blocks apart.
    There is a bike store between the boys' houses.
    The bike store is 5 blocks from David's house.
    How far is the bike store from Carlos' house?

    Answer _____ blocks.

19. Jane walked 5 blocks to Sara's house.
    Both girls walked 3 blocks to the pool.
    How many blocks in all did Jane walk?

    Answer _____ blocks.

CHAPTER 3 Extra Practice

▶ Add.

pages 46–47			
1. 37 + 26	2. 48 + 19	3. 25 + 58	4. 58 + 37
pages 48–51			
5. 164 + 153	6. 276 + 183	7. 4,293 + 2,803	8. 6,737 + 2,912

▶ Subtract.

pages 52–53			
9. 54 − 28	10. 72 − 44	11. 37 − 19	12. 43 − 26
pages 54–57			
13. 752 − 431	14. 823 − 315	15. 6,382 − 3,291	16. 7,591 − 4,485

▶ Write each time.   pages 58–59

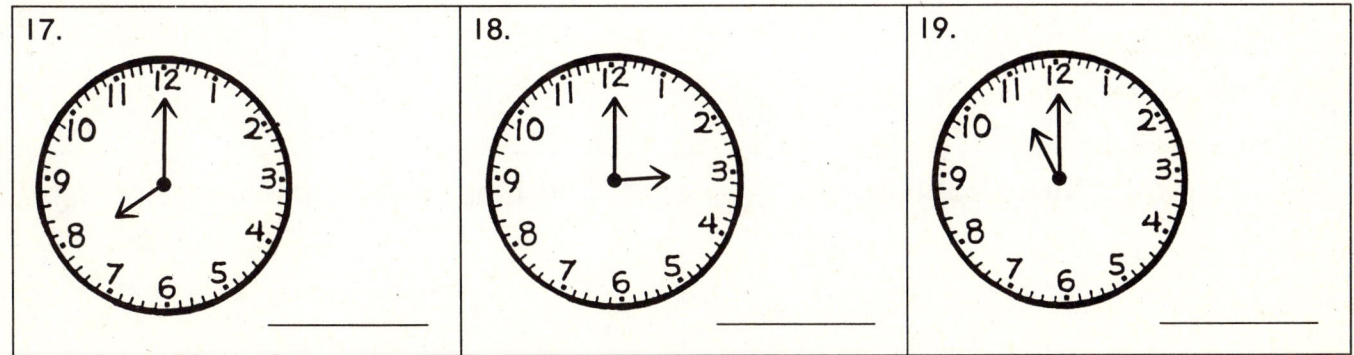

151

CHAPTER 3 Extra Practice

Tim and Cora went to the beach.
The table shows what they saw.

Seen at the Beach

	Crabs	Fish	Clams	Starfish	Shells	Seagulls
Tim	13	29	6	3	26	19
Cora	20	17	12	5	14	25

▶ Use the table to answer. pages 60–61

20. How many crabs in all did they see? + ____ _____ crabs	21. How many shells in all did they see? + ____ _____ shells
22. How many clams in all did they see? + ____ _____ clams	23. How many seagulls in all did they see? + ____ _____ seagulls
24. How many fish in all did they see? + ____ _____ fish	25. How many starfish in all did they see? + ____ _____ starfish
26. Who saw more seagulls? _____	27. Did Cora see more clams or fish? more _____

152

CHAPTER 4 **Extra Practice**

▶ Multiply.

pages 76–79

1. 5
   × 2

2. 8
   × 2

3. 7
   × 3

4. 9
   × 3

pages 80–81

5. 6
   × 4

6. 4
   × 4

7. 9
   × 4

8. 8
   × 4

pages 82–83

9. 4
   × 5

10. 7
   × 5

11. 5
   × 5

12. 8
   × 5

pages 84–85

13. 8
   × 0

14. 9
   × 1

15. 1
   × 0

16. 3
   × 1

▶ Draw the hands on each clock to show the time. pages 88–89

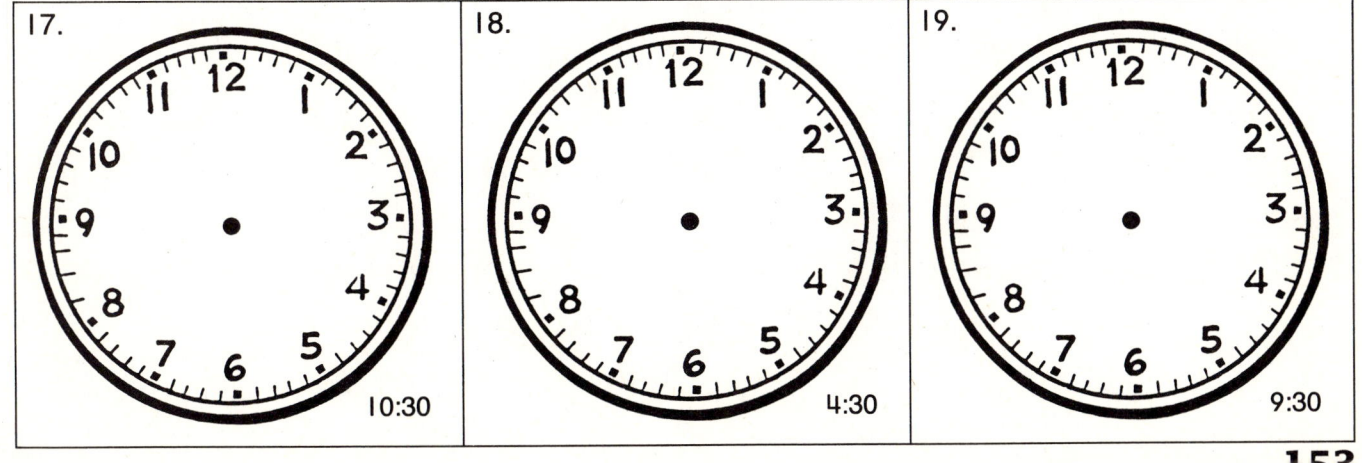

17. 10:30

18. 4:30

19. 9:30

153

CHAPTER  **Extra Practice**

▶ Write numbers to make the tables. pages 90–91

20. Ed bought a key chain for 2¢.
    How much will 2, 3, and 4 key chains cost?

Key Chain Prices

Key Chains	1	2	3	4
Cost	2¢	___¢	___¢	___¢

21. Gloria bought a ring for 4¢.
    How much will 2, 3, and 4 rings cost?

Ring Prices

Rings	1	2	3	4
Cost	4¢	___¢	___¢	___¢

22. Ying paid 6¢ for a hat.
    How much will 2, 3, and 4 hats cost?

Hat Prices

Hats	1	2	3	4
Cost	6¢	___¢	___¢	___¢

23. Oscar bought a pair of sunglasses for 7¢.
    How much will 2, 3, and 4 pairs of sunglasses cost?

Sunglasses Prices

Sunglasses	1	2	3	4
Cost	7¢	___¢	___¢	___¢

24. Sue paid for 9¢ for a belt.
    How much will 2, 3, 4, and 5 belts cost?

Belt Prices

Belts	1	2	3	4	5
Cost	9¢	___¢	___¢	___¢	___¢

CHAPTER 5 Extra Practice

▶ Multiply.

pages 98–99 1. 1 × 6	2. 5 × 6	3. 7 × 6	4. 9 × 6
pages 100–101 5. 4 × 7	6. 9 × 7	7. 8 × 7	8. 7 × 7
pages 102–103 9. 4 × 8	10. 9 × 8	11. 5 × 8	12. 8 × 8
pages 104–105 13. 3 × 9	14. 7 × 9	15. 6 × 9	16. 9 × 9

▶ Write each time.   pages 110–111

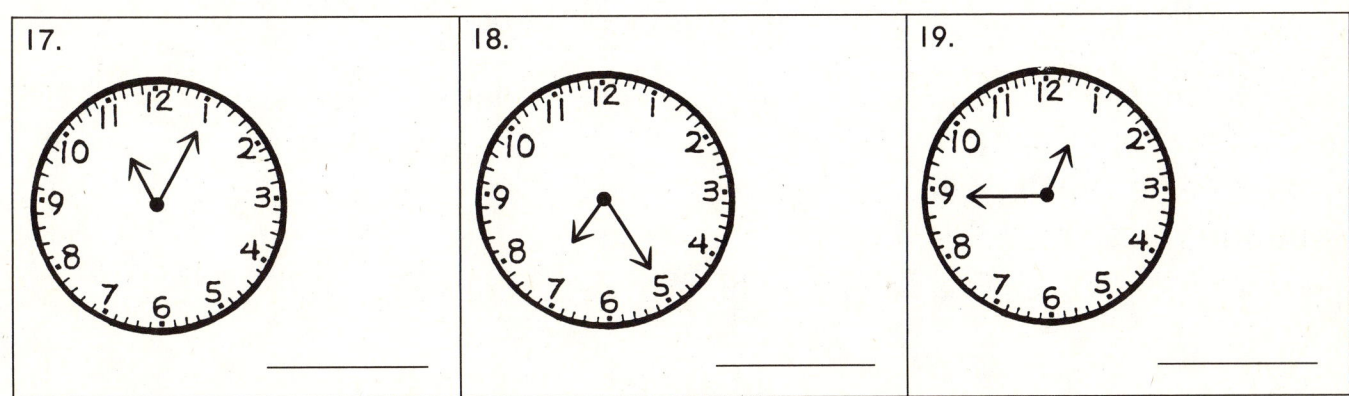

155

CHAPTER 5 Extra Practice

▸ Find the rule in each pattern.
Write the next number. pages 112–113

20. | 5 | 6 | 7 | 8 | |

The rule is _____.

21. | 24 | 23 | 22 | 21 | |

The rule is _____.

22. | 12 | 14 | 16 | 18 | |

The rule is _____.

23. | 12 | 18 | 24 | 30 | |

The rule is _____.

24. | 21 | 19 | 17 | 15 | |

The rule is _____.

25. | 15 | 20 | 25 | 30 | |

The rule is _____.

26. | 30 | 40 | 50 | 60 | |

The rule is _____.

27. | 35 | 30 | 25 | 20 | |

The rule is _____.

28. | 0 | 6 | 12 | 18 | |

The rule is _____.

29. | 8 | 16 | 24 | 32 | |

The rule is _____.

▸ Make your own patterns.
Write the rules.

30. | | | | | |

The rule is _____.

31. | | | | | |

The rule is _____.

156

CHAPTER 6 Extra Practice

▶ Divide.

pages 120–123			
1. 2)8	2. 2)16	3. 3)12	4. 3)21
pages 124–125			
5. 4)12	6. 4)32	7. 4)20	8. 4)36
pages 126–127			
9. 5)35	10. 5)40	11. 5)45	12. 5)25
pages 128–129			
13. 6)36	14. 6)42	15. 6)30	16. 6)54

▶ Match.   pages 132–133

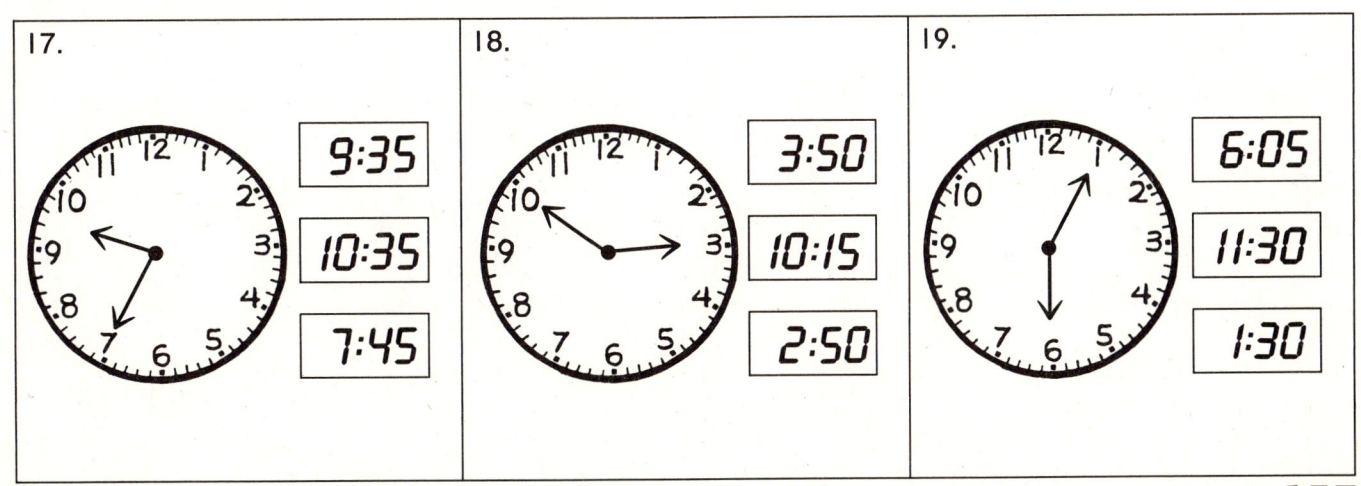

157

CHAPTER 6 Extra Practice

▶ Find the rule in each pattern. Write the next number. pages 134–135

20. | 3 | 6 |
     | 4 | 8 |
     | 5 | |
The rule is ____.

21. | 2 | 6 |
     | 3 | 9 |
     | 4 | |
The rule is ____.

22. | 8 | 4 |
     | 10 | 5 |
     | 12 | |
The rule is ____.

23. | 12 | 12 |
     | 13 | 13 |
     | 14 | |
The rule is ____.

24. | 2 | 10 |
     | 3 | 15 |
     | 4 | |
The rule is ____.

25. | 10 | 1 |
     | 20 | 2 |
     | 30 | |
The rule is ____.

26. | 6 | 1 |
     | 12 | 2 |
     | 18 | |
The rule is ____.

27. | 1 | 6 |
     | 2 | 12 |
     | 3 | |
The rule is ____.

28. | 3 | 12 |
     | 4 | 16 |
     | 5 | |
The rule is ____.

29. | 12 | 4 |
     | 15 | 5 |
     | 18 | |
The rule is ____.

▶ Find the rule in each pattern. Write the next number pair.

30. | 1 | 6 |
     | 2 | 12 |
     | 3 | 18 |
The rule is ____.

31. | 2 | 6 |
     | 3 | 9 |
     | 4 | 12 |
The rule is ____.